Insight Solutions

Creative Problem-Solving

Insight Solutions

Creative Problem-Solving

Sort Out The S.P.I.C.E^3
FIDGET And RELAX

Gary R. Ford MBA, PhD

Insight Solutions
Creative Problem-Solving

Published by Insight Publishers
Address: Thorsby, Alberta, Canada
Website: http//garyrford.ca/insight
Edited, designed and typeset by the Author
Printed in the United States of America or Canada
ISBN: 978-1-7750699-0-4

DEDICATION

Dedicated to all of you who want to increase your general effectiveness in life and to see opportunities where others fail to look; to all people who want to achieve greater problem-solving performance at work, in relationships, and during play.

Table Of Contents

Preface

As an instructor of creative problem-solving workshops, I noticed frequent occurrences of behaviors that limit personal effectiveness:

- ignoring problems and problem-solving opportunities,

- regarding problems as weaknesses that are to be ignored, put up with, denied, or worked around as opposed to dealt with,

- giving divided attention to problem-solving while "multi-tasking" or otherwise distracted,

- using problem-solving behavior that is too often disorganized and inefficient,

- going off on tangents considering different possibilities before properly understanding the problem that is to be solved,

- rejecting ideas that could become good solutions just because the ideas are unusual, mis-understood, expressed poorly, or were expressed by someone that is not regarded as credible,

- letting confusion about where one is within the problem-solving process cause frustration and quitting,

- settling for compromise solutions more often than optimum solutions and seldom pursuing exceptional results,

- arriving at decisions that fail to be implemented,

- settling back into a status quo with less than adequate results because problem-solving efforts failed, and

- seeing opportunities as something that fortuitously emerge as opposed to something that can be created.

Individual and group performance is seldom better than average, and only a few people seem to achieve outstanding results. People working together on problems often experience confusion about what the other person is doing, frustration, discouragement and even conflict as the participants try to find mutually acceptable solutions.

We know enough about what effective problem-solving looks like that all of this doesn't have to be. We know the appropriate attitudes, thinking processes, and behavioral skills that result in effective problem-solving. We know an organized sequence of steps that effectively move a problem-solver through the creative and critical thinking processes that yield successful solutions. All of this can be learned, and in doing so, personal, couple, group and organizational performance can be improved.

During my post-graduate studies in business administration, psychology, and change management, and during a work history that included training individuals, couples, and work groups in how-to skills for effective problem-solving, I came to better understand what it takes to arrive at exceptional results when problem-solving or examining new opportunities. This book shares what I have learned.

Introduction

Be more effective in life by enhancing your effectiveness at solving problems – big and small. You have an opportunity to pursue excellence by using specific skills and following a sequential process to realize optimal results.

In this modern world, we don't have problems. "Problem" is seen to be a dirty word. In our current lexicon, we tend to have opportunities, difficulties, frustrations, hiccups in our plans, roadblocks or challenges instead. These neutralizing terms often allow us to ignore the fact that there are gaps between the way things are, and the way we wish they could be. These are actually problems, and could be effectively resolved if we applied an effective problem-solving process.

> **Problem** = a gap between the way things are and the way we want them to be.

You've lived a life full of such gaps. For the most part you figured out how to close many of them. Although you've had to ignore some of your problems for lack of knowing how to deal with them, you've been problem-solving all your life. In your own way, you are likely as competent at problem-solving as most everyone else.

However, have you had any times in your life where you just felt stuck. You knew that you wanted something to be better than it was but just couldn't, at that moment in time anyway, figure out how to achieve what you wanted. You might have floundered about, frustrated because you knew you had a problem, but for whatever reason, the usual ways of dealing with it didn't work.

Perhaps there have been times in your life where others were telling you that you had a problem but you just couldn't see it. Maybe you were receiving critical comments from a spouse, a boss, a long time friend and these comments hurt but just didn't register as a problem you could do something about. You may have felt stuck in an unhappy place but weren't even able to conceive of the situation as a solvable problem.

You may know people for whom new opportunities and life success seemed to come easily. Perhaps you've wondered why they seem so fortunate, so lucky while you seem somewhat handicapped in your own pursuit of life improvement. Yes, some people are luckier and win the lottery of life. However, others are more successful because they are better problem-solvers, confidently seeking out and resolving issues before they become crises and looking for new opportunities for growth.

It's my guess that when you feel stuck, you can't think about how you're problem-solving because you usually just do it, reflexively, even unconsciously. Like most people, you probably aren't even sure how you approach and solve problems. Problem-solving is just something we do but can't readily say how. Test this assumption out.

Take a sheet of paper and write out the process that you follow when you solve problems. What are the steps that you take to come up with and then apply a solution? How do you know when to engage in problem-solving? When you do, how do you do it? How do you know when you've found the best solution? Just write a list of all the thoughts that come to mind. Notice how easy or difficult it is to write this stuff down.

Now think back. When were you taught how to problem-solve? Did you learn your method in school? Alternatively, was problem-solving a skill set that was passed to you by some mentor such as a parent, teacher, elder in the family, elder in the community, a friend? Or did you just somehow develop your own way as you grew up?

We think you probably learned to solve problems on your own. Life presented itself. You were confronted by wanting something you didn't have, and you had to figure out how to get it. You generally did this without even thinking you were problem-solving. The way you solve your own problems became a subconscious process, one that was available to use when you needed it.

Conscious = the thoughts, sensations, feelings, memories, and needs that we are aware of; we are using our conscious mind when our mind is aware of what it's thinking, experiencing, and doing.

Subconscious = occurring below conscious awareness; our brain is performing without our having to consciously think about it, or storing memories, knowledge, and skills that aren't currently in our awareness (sometimes referred to as unconscious operation within our brain).

This is true for most of us. So how easy was it to write out your own problem-solving process? If you found that you could clearly list the steps, describe the process, and articulate what you do each step of the way, then it is both a conscious and unconscious skill set for you. That deserves congratulations because it is an ability that most people do not have.

If however, you found it difficult to clearly describe the mechanics of your own problem-solving, then this suggests that it is only an unconscious skill set. This is more normal. For most people, how they solve problems is a subconscious process, something that happens below their awareness, mostly a mystery to their conscious mind, and something that they can't easily articulate.

Generally, you've probably done quite well using your own particular way of approaching problems. You've probably had moments in time where you just couldn't figure out what to do. But then, somehow you figured your way through the confusion, and moved on to what you wanted to achieve. There were likely experiences where you didn't get what you wanted, but overall, you've been doing okay. If pressed, you would probably say that life is going well, and yes there are a few dissatisfactions but they aren't all that much bother.

How about the people around you? Are they doing okay solving their own problems? Or do you see some people struggling, not achieving what they really want? Are those close to you fully satisfied that they can close their own gaps between the way things are and the way they want them to be? What do you notice about their problem-solving behavior? Does it seem organized, logical, structured or more impulsive, haphazard, inconsistent, troubled?

What happens when you have to problem-solve with others? Remember when you had to do school assignments with a classmate. Did such assignments go smoothly or were there conflicts between the two or three of you? What happens when you and your spouse attempt to tackle a problem that the two of you share? Any conflicts?

At work, if you have to work in a team setting, what happens during a meeting when a problem is identified? Does discussion go smoothly, with a clear solution produced and effective action taken to close the gap, or does talk seem to be a waste of time and the problem lingers because no effective action is taken?

Perhaps, your experience is similar to that of most people. Solving problems with others doesn't go as smoothly as it could. Meetings don't go well. Participants often wish they could work on their own. Problems don't get resolved. Sometimes it might appear that the group has worked well together to come up with a solution, but that solution doesn't get implemented; or if implemented, not the way that everyone expected, thereby achieving different results than intended.

When you problem-solve with others, and experience difficulties working together, is it because you disagree about possible solutions; or is it because you disagree over how to get the darn problem solved? If you've developed your own problem-solving approach, but can't quite articulate just exactly how you do it; and if everyone else has developed their own problem-solving approach, but can't quite articulate just exactly how they do it; it makes sense that team work is fraught with tension as the participants unintentionally compete over which way to solve the problem.

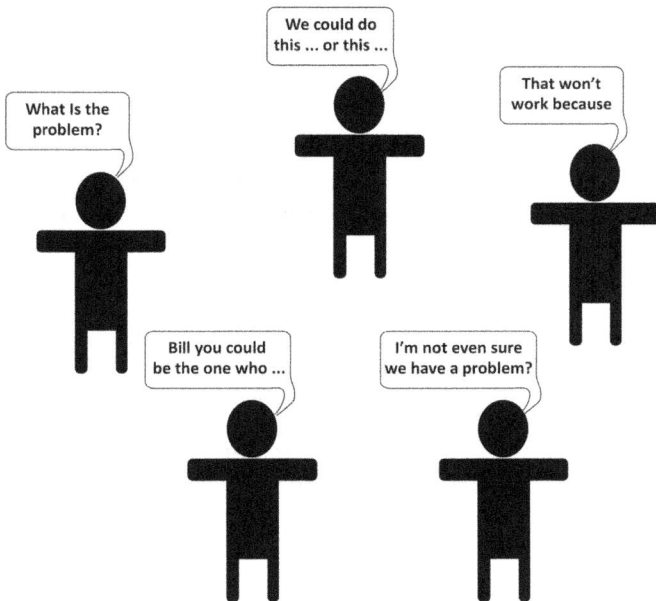

Few teams, and even fewer couples or families sit down and discuss what approach to take when solving problems. If you have five different team members working on a problem without first discussing and arriving at an agreed upon problem-solving process, then each person will be tackling the problem in his or her own way.

One person will be trying to figure out just exactly what the problem is, while another might be thinking of how to solve the problem, coming up with one or more solution ideas. A third might be thinking exactly how a specific solution should be implemented, while a fourth might be arguing what is wrong with each idea. The fifth might not even realize that the others are working to solve a problem because he or she doesn't have any awareness that one exists. He or she might be thinking that things are fine just the way they are.

Similarly, if your discussions as a couple break out into disagreements, it may look like the conflict is about opposing points of view; but much of the conflict is likely because of an unintentional and likely subconscious competition over whose problem-solving method will be used to deal with the current problem. You want to solve the problem using your process and your partner wants to use the one he or she knows and trusts. This is normal, but most people don't realize that this is what the fight is actually about.

To some degree, the underlying issue is power and who controls the process. But enmeshed within that struggle, the two participants are unaware that each approaches problem-solving differently. Because they haven't specifically thought about how each of them deals with problems, they aren't able to effectively talk about how to approach a problem they share.

Because of this unintentional conflict over how to problem-solve with another person, or several people at once, many people prefer to tackle problems on their own. If we let the individual team members go off to do so, or if two spouses work on a problem separately, we might get completely different definitions of the problem, and very different suggestions as to the solution. This, in itself, might not be a bad thing if the different possibilities could be discussed cooperatively and effectively. However, if we need all of the participants to implement the same solution with conviction, it's not going to happen.

Because there has been no deliberate learning of a sequence of steps, our own problem-solving process is likely weaker than it could be. Most of us need a clearer, more efficient, more effective way to shift from realization that there is a gap between what we want and what we have, to a place we want to be.

Most people tend to have only general answers to the question – "How do you solve your problems?" When talking about problem-solving some people say ideas just emerge if we pay attention. Others might say we think laterally. Some say solutions come from the right brain, when we put the conscious mind to sleep. Some make pro and con lists and the answer just comes. There are many euphemisms for generating solutions to life's problems. However, what we really do is much more complex and worth discovering.

So, what can be done about these issues? How can we achieve better problem-solving success as an individual? What can a couple do to solve problems more effectively? How can we achieve better outcomes when solving problems within a group?

The answer is to think very deliberately about problem-solving as a learnable skill set - a set of specific behaviors that leads to effective problem-solving, both for individuals, couples and for groups. These behaviors can be studied and learned. Put together, these skills are called a problem-solving process. There is benefit to learning an organized and well developed problem-solving approach.

Looking at all of the comments and ideas that people have generated about effective problem-solving, we can organize the information into a series of steps that can be taken to arrive at effective solutions. This book presents a problem-solving sequence with detailed skills that can be used each step of the way to arrive at more effective problem solution. This process is offered to show how to arrive at high quality solutions and effective implementation.

The goal is not to convince you to adopt this approach but to give you a clear foil against which to think through your own problem-solving behavior and to give you a language you can use with others to identify how each of you solves problems. When problem-solving with someone else, you will then be able to create a shared approach that both of you agree will be followed when tackling shared problems.

If you sharpen your own problem-solving approach, and work with your significant problem-solving participants to develop a shared approach, your results will improve. More importantly, problem-solving will be fun. If problem-solving is fun, you will do more of it and your life will become more effective.

You will move from dealing with crises to looking for new opportunities. Dealing with catastrophe is very taxing but dealing with exciting new possibilities is life enriching. Your success in life, and your overall satisfaction will rise as you improve your problem-solving prowess.

> Throughout this book, the term problem-solver is used to refer to an individual, couple or group that wants to close the gap between the way things are and the way they really want them to be.

Understanding Change

Solving problems and pursuing new opportunities is about change. How you feel about change will seriously affect your willingness to pursue new and better results in both life and work, and affect your overall personal effectiveness. In order to be a better problem-solver, you need to understand how one gets ready to make a change and train yourself toward greater readiness. You will increase your effectiveness by adopting an attitude of welcoming change. You want to become your own change agent.

Insight Potential When Welcoming Change – *Once you open your mind to the potential for change, you will see new opportunities for improvement in everything around you. You will be able to be a more intentional problem-solver. Growth and development will accelerate for you and you will increase your chances for greater success.*

Problem-solving is about how we manage change. Typically, we resist change, preferring to keep things stable, reliable, the same. We want things to be what we are most used to. It seems that we are wired to try to stay comfortable, consistent, safe and this means resisting change. Flux can be uncomfortable, uncertain, and feel unsafe. We want our world to stay predictable so we strive to keep it so. We strive to maintain our status quo

Our status quo is the existing state or condition, the way things are now. Readiness for change is based on three different emotional states relative to the way things are now. There can be times when we're quite comfortable and satisfied with the way things are, times when we might feel very frustrated with some aspect of the way things are, and even times when we want something more than we currently have.

Readiness For Change

		State	Common Emotions	Intentions
GREEN	GO Zone	Ready for Change	Eagerness, Excitement, Expectations,	We know what we can do, so let's do it.
YELLOW	WAIT Zone	Accepting Status Quo	Calm, Comfortable, Accepting	Let's just stay the same.
RED	STOP Zone	Stuck and Pained	Loss, Frustration, Irritation, Anxiousness	We really need to do something but can't.

A person can be in a state of high readiness for change (the green "GO" zone) where he or she really wants something new, or in a state that is simple acceptance of the current situation (the yellow "WAIT" zone), or in a state of feeling stuck and pained in some way (the red "STOP" zone) because the way things are now aren't at all what the person wants.

10

Much of what most people think about as problem-solving is actually work they do to try to maintain their status quo. As nothing stays the same for very long, this can be self-defeating activity. Instead, our effectiveness in life rises when we embrace change, growth and development. Typically, we become something better when we look for better results, a higher level of performance, something more.

But because of our psychological processes, we can easily ignore or deny opportunities to problem-solve and to pursue new and better results. Our normal human inclination is to get into and stay in the "WAIT" zone. We associate this with comfort, satisfaction, acceptance of what we have. This place is presumed to be stress free and we adapt in little ways to keep it that way. In such an emotional state, we choose not to face and look at the unpleasant, disappointing, or frustrating aspects of our world. Our attitude is "Let's just stay the same."

However, even when we accept things the way they are, we likely have problems within our status quo. In fact, it's safe to say there are always problems within a given status quo – most are small, but potentially some are big. However, to maintain a state of comfort (the "WAIT" zone), we have the capacity to subconsciously deny either the existence or consequence of the problems. It's as if our brain functions to keep us in a state of equilibrium by denying or covering over any reasons to change. It's as if we unconsciously think to ourselves, "This is just the way things are."

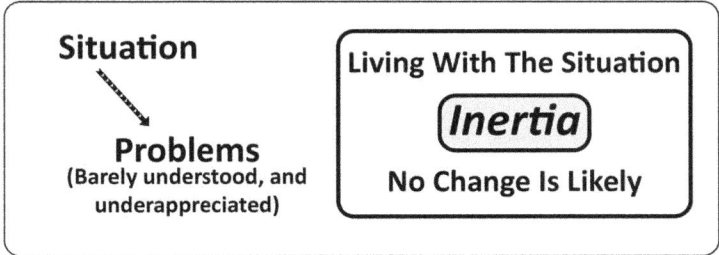

Problems have symptoms, many of which we ignore. In some cases, we might acknowledge some minor symptoms while ignoring major ones. It's as if the minor symptoms distract us, and we give ourselves permission to think they're acceptable so we have no reason to change.

This ability is so inherent that we can accept serious symptoms as just normal. In paying attention to only some of our symptoms, we often fail to interpret what our problems really are. Too often, we think we have one problem when we actually have another.

If we allow awareness of the real problem to surface, it's likely we will downplay the significance of the problem – "Yes, it can be frustrating when that happens, but it's no big deal." To minimize the significance of our problems, we ignore the consequences or treat the costs of the problems as inconsequential. By doing so, we minimize our motivation to make any sort of change.

In turn, new opportunities might present themselves, but to pursue them would mean giving up what is predictable, safe, comfortable. Even the promise of great benefits that might be realized by acting on the opportunity can be ignored by focusing on the great risks that would have to be taken and the potential for failure. This ability is also so inherent that we can often ignore great opportunities.

If directed to explore the implications of those problems or missed opportunities, we confront the real costs and lost benefits – both tangible and intangible.

Tangible Costs	What we currently pay to do what we do. These costs have clear financial measures.
Intangible Costs	Costs that may be more emotional than dollar based, or dollar based costs where it is hard to accurately measure the financial implications. Intangible costs include the negative emotions we live with, the needs that go unsatisfied, the benefits (known and unknown) that we don't get to experience.

The simple insight that things could be better precipitates awareness of the real costs of not making a change, of doing nothing new to bring about different results. If people don't acknowledge and truly experience these tangible and intangible costs, they're likely to prefer the status quo over change.

However, when a person focuses on the implications or consequences of the problems or missed opportunities, he or she begins to realize there are some painful negative feelings. Realizing how much the status quo actually costs can induce some degree of emotional discomfort, becoming a catalyst for change. This could be experienced as disappointment, irritation, frustration, exasperation, even the more intense emotional pain of loss, regret, and grief; or just simply a state of wanting better results. That acknowledgment of the degree of negative feelings comes as an insight – the problem is worse than previously thought.

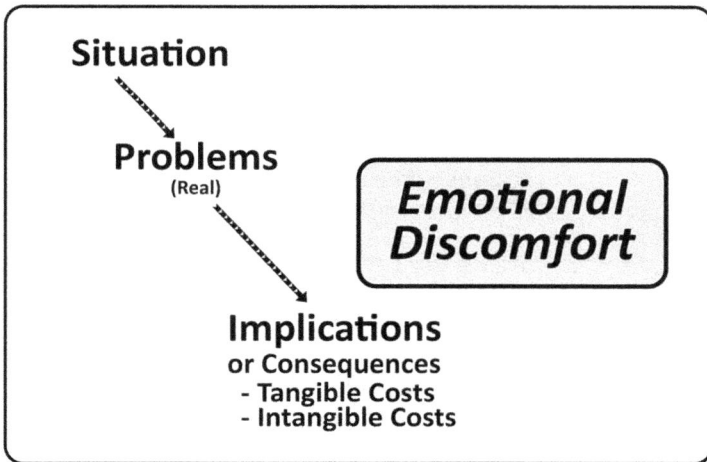

Change is an emotional process, often involving some degree of discomfort. This is why people generally avoid change. However, once these emotions are triggered by the insight as to how serious the problems really are, how much they actually cost, people want to change. When a person can't ignore the costs any longer, he or she itches for change. This person likely won't change yet, but will begin to think seriously about needing something different.

Even though people know they have problems with significant consequences, they often don't change because they feel constrained, prevented in some way from making things better. They tend to become aware of the constraints they believe block their ability to make that change.

This results in discouragement, frustration, perhaps hopelessness and despair if the costs are high and the roadblocks are seen as insurmountable (*being in the red "STOP" or stuck zone*). We call this awareness of the costs and constraints the Reality Trough – the person realizes the low point of his or her current situation.

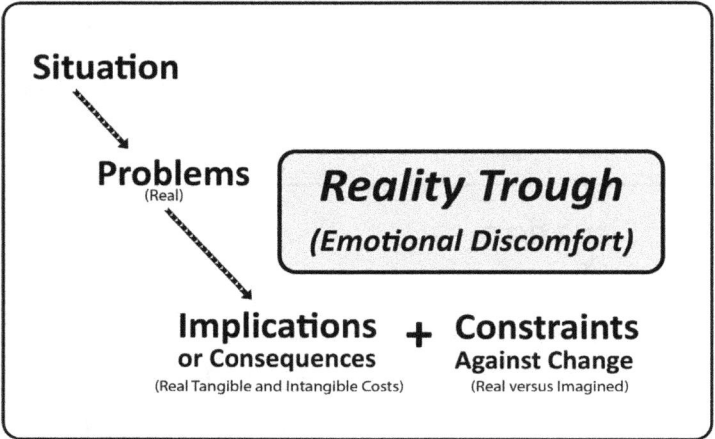

Situation

Problems
(Real)

Reality Trough
(Emotional Discomfort)

Implications + **Constraints**
or Consequences   Against Change
(Real Tangible and Intangible Costs)   (Real versus Imagined)

Some of these constraints will be real. As such, change is only possible if the solution overcomes or removes the constraint. However, we also tend to imagine constraints. For example, these imaginary roadblocks could be a perceived lack of resources, even though we may have what it will take to make the change. Or the imagined roadblocks could be arbitrary rules we somehow impose on ourselves, even though there is no other person or force putting these rules in place. Alternatively, we might feel blocked because we have a belief we aren't physically or emotionally capable of effectively making the change, despite evidence to the contrary.

Once perceived constraints are really explored, people become more aware of which are real, and which are imagined. Sometimes, just thinking about their excuses while facing the real costs of not changing will cause people to realize the reasons aren't limiting after all. Upon this realization, the imagined constraints can be set aside. Once a person does this, the solution only has to overcome the real constraints.

Instead of denial, the person confronts the reality of his or her own situation and experiences the related emotions. In this emotional state, a person is likely to be on the lookout for how things could be made better. Once a person actually wonders how things can get better, new expectations begin to emerge.

He or she starts to form minimal expectations as to what change would have to deliver. These minimal expectations are seldom much of a reach beyond what the person already has and seldom involve any significant form of perceptual shift. In its simplest form, the person may wonder if a small change would accomplish enough gain to be worth undergoing. In other words, the first inclination is to just tweak the status quo so that we don't have to undergo dramatic change to get better. This person sets his or her goals relatively low. At this stage, the motivation to change also remains low.

However, if a person dwells on what he or she would **really** like to achieve and manages to reframe his or her thinking around new wants and desires, then excitement grows.

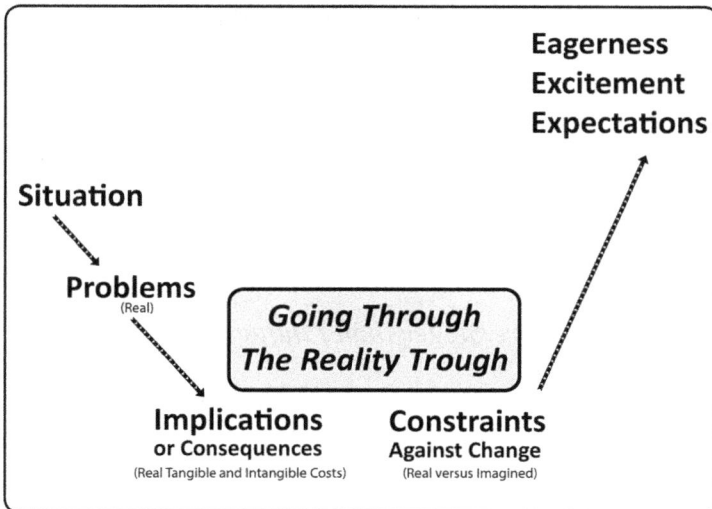

This shift happens most effectively when the person starts to wonder, "If I figured out an ideal solution, what significantly better results could I really achieve?" With new insights about the additional results that could be achieved, the person becomes eager for change.

It's imperative that the much better results appear achievable. The person may initially be hesitant to reframe his or her thinking into a desire for greater results, believing the better results aren't achievable. He or she may even second guess his or her right to hold such desires. But if an individual can come to think the higher-order goal is achievable and okay for him or her to want, he or she will make a dramatic paradigm shift accompanied by growing excitement. He or she will no longer want to settle for what he or she currently has.

From this excitement, the person moves to an eagerness to find a way to make things better. Instead of wanting to stay the same, the person really wants to achieve a different and better outcome.

At this point, the person is much more likely to go after what he or she really wants. He or she may do this in small ways, like just listening to whatever relevant information comes into his or her world, in moderate ways by trying to engage in subconscious problem-solving, or in big ways such as initiating serious problem-solving efforts and a search for a truly valuable solution.

Readiness For Change

To get ready for change, the person's thinking must go from:

"Things are okay the way they are."

to

"Well, I'm frustrated by… but I can live with it."

through

"I guess the costs are bigger than I thought."

and

"I can't do anything because…."

to

"You mean things really could be better?

to

"Wow! The benefits would be….".

and finally to

"How do I do this?"

This understanding of change applies to businesses as well as individuals. When a business fails to focus on the full implications of its current manner of doing business, and the tangible and intangible costs within its business model, that business will put up with many problems. If the business does not question its constraints and search for new opportunities, it will stay stuck. If it doesn't feel the need to bring about a change to achieve better results, it won't change. Just as individuals must encounter their Reality Trough, businesses and corporate systems need to move through the same change cycle.

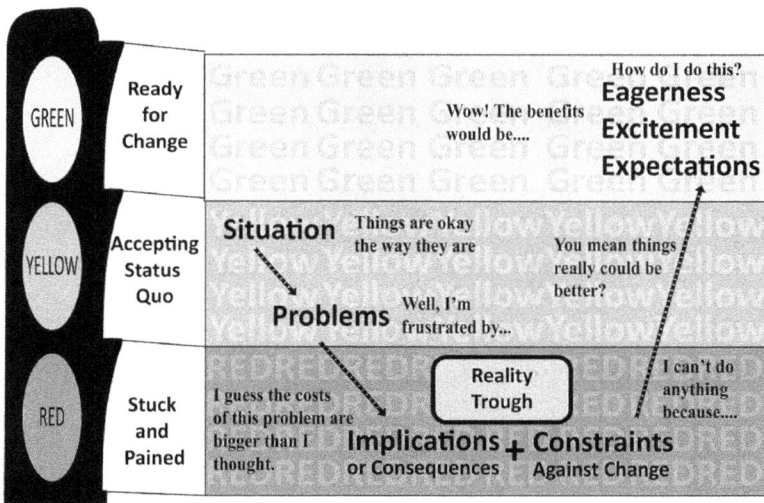

This exploration of the real costs of the problems, the discovery of the real constraints, and consideration of what could ideally be achieved, involves going through the Reality Trough to reach an eager, excited state of readiness for change. We call this insight process, the S.P.I.C.E.[3] Sequence:

- **S**ituation or status quo,
- **P**roblems,
- **I**mplications of those problems,
- **C**onstraints, and

- Expectations, Excitement and Eagerness.

When people gain insight as they explore their own S.P.I.C.E[3], they're increasingly ready to undergo change. They have a clear hope things can be better, and a drive to achieve that outcome.

An individual, couple or business has to move from the comfort of his or her status quo, travel through the Reality Trough to confront the implications of staying the same, bump up against what he or she believes to be roadblocks, and then consider what could be gained if a change is made. This process moves the individual, couple or organization into the "GO" zone. People really want change when in the green "GO" zone. Actual change occurs once the person, couple or organization achieves readiness, engages in problem-solving, and clearly finds a solution to real problems and new opportunities.

Giving up the familiar for something new has both tangible and emotional costs. The person, couple or organization experiencing these costs and emotions must come to believe the new state, and the gain to be had, is worth the price of change. If the problem-solver does this, he or she moves awareness from the yellow caution ("WAIT") zone, through the painful red ("STOP") zone, to the highly positive and exciting green ("GO") zone. A problem-solver has to arrive here in order to be eager enough to pursue a solution and make a change.

Emotional States That Inhibit Problem-Solving

There are four particular emotional states that can inhibit or interfere with problem-solving:

- being satisfied with the way things are,

- feeling discouraged and experiencing a lack of hope that things can get better,

- holding onto a general resistance to change, and

- feeling an eagerness for change but having a lack of appreciation for what the real problem is.

SATISFACTION WITH THE WAY THINGS ARE

This is the most common emotional state that we have to overcome if we wish to increase our own personal effectiveness and accomplishments. It is all too normal that people are relatively passive and complacent about gaps between the way things are and the way they want things to be. There is no perceived need to engage in problem-solving.

If an individual, couple or business doesn't experience any pain or see any benefits from change, a preference to stay the same will exist. There is no motivation to look for a new solution because things are fine the way they are. The problems and their implications are not believed to be significant and in this situation, there's just not enough excitement for change. The value of change is believed to be too small.

Problem Solver Prefers The Status Quo

No Perceived Value to Change - Not Enough
Awareness of the Costs and No Expected Gain

The problem-solver must be willing to think about and identify the existence of real problem(s). With greater clarity about the problem(s), the person would then need to calculate the costs of these symptoms, issues and problems in order to recognize that change would be better.

The problem-solver must achieve a deeper awareness of the reality of his or her situation and the corresponding emotions that have been suppressed through the process of denial. The individual must come to terms with what is real. This has to be accomplished before the individual might even consider doing something different. The problem-solver, either individual, couple or group, must facilitate insight about the real problem and develop a heightened awareness of the real costs and degree of actual pain.

From the emotions of a deep Reality Trough, the problem-solver must then consider what could be achieved if an ideal new solution could be identified. It helps if the problem-solver can imagine what new results could be achieved if a miracle could occur. The problem-solver needs to develop a belief that new, higher-order benefits can be realized if change is made.

DISCOURAGED – WITH LOW HOPE FOR GAIN

In some cases, an individual, couple or organization may know the real costs and feel the true degree of pain within his or her status quo, but hold a belief that there is nothing that can be done about the problem(s). Likely, such a person, couple or group has thoughts about fixing the problem but does not yet believe the problem(s) can be resolved. There may be a perception that certain constraints block positive change. Perhaps lacking any knowledge of what better results could be achieved, there is no vision of a better way to be.

Low Hope For Gain

GREEN	Ready for Change	
YELLOW	Accepting Status Quo	Situation / Eagerness Excitement Expectations
		Problems
RED	Stuck and Pained	Enough Reality Trough To Feel Discomfort But Not High Enough Expected Benefits
		Implications + Constraints or Consequences Against Change

Perceived Value To Be Gained Is Too Low

Wants Change Badly But Doesn't Yet See Any Potential Gain From A Change

This problem-solver is likely going to feel very frustrated and lack hope things can get better. He or she will feel stuck in the painful "STOP" zone, wanting change badly, but not yet seeing the possibility of change. In this place, the problem-solver is stuck in his or her current way of looking at the world with blinders on, preventing a new perception of the better way things could be.

The problem-solver has to develop new ways of thinking about what could be achieved. The problem-solver must challenge his or her own perception of the constraints and elevate his or her expectations.

The problem-solver needs to shift his or her focus from the painful emotions to ponder what benefits could be experienced if the problem(s) could be solved. The problem-solver needs to address the question, "If an ideal solution existed, what could be accomplished?"

In doing this, a shift in perception is brought about. Instead of dwelling on what can't be achieved, the problem-solver is inspired to consider new results. Instead of hopeless thinking, the problem-solver shifts to hopeful thoughts. From there, the problem-solver can imagine what would be gained if he or she could find the right solution. The problem-solver becomes excited about those benefits, and eager to make a change.

RESISTANCE

For some reason, a problem-solver might have a strong prejudice against what he or she believes to be too much change and hold a more passionate commitment to keeping things the same. This person behaves like a bulldog that has locked its jaws onto a stick and just won't let go. Any effort to persuade the letting go is usually ignored or rebuffed.

An individual, couple or organization might have an inkling something new is needed but just hold a general resistance to making any sort of change. Or the problem-solver may close off all awareness of issues, ignore all problem symptoms and hold a "pollyanna" view of the world in order to maintain harmony.

An unreasonable or illogical satisfaction with the way things are can prevent some individuals, couples and groups from engaging in problem-solving. Something must be done to remove these blinders, to get the problem-solver to explore his or her own reality. It may take an outsider's intervention, or a catastrophic event to force the problem-solver to examine his or her S.P.I.C.E.[3]. It would be more effective if such persons could adopt a more open orientation to change.

EAGERNESS COUPLED WITH A LACK OF APPRECIATION FOR THE REAL PROBLEM

Some problem-solvers are just too eager to experience change. They have an unusually high attraction to new experience. However, such problem-solvers have to be careful to prevent getting seduced into believing that they have a clear and full awareness of their own S.P.I.C.E^3. Such a problem-solver has to confront his or her own impatience to bring about change because change just for change's sake is just as likely to reduce personal effectiveness as it is to bring about a change for the better.

This eager problem-solver may know he or she has a problem and know what that problem is. However, this problem-solver may not yet fully appreciate what the problem costs or what a solution has to deliver in terms of improved results. In turn, there may not be sufficient understanding of the potential benefits he or she wants to achieve. This will mean a lower incentive to find an optimum solution.

This problem-solver must break free of any assumption that he or she doesn't have to take time to expand awareness of his or her S.P.I.C.E^3. The happy, excited, and eager problem-solver needs to back up and explore his or her Reality Trough, thereby feeling the troubled emotions associated with the real costs and constraints, before pursuing change.

The Reality Trough

In order for each of the "satisfied", "too eager", "discouraged", or "resistant" problem-solvers to bring about effective change, they must learn how to move into and through the Reality Trough. An individual, couple, group, or organization needs to fully experience the reality of the problem in order to generate sufficient motivation to reach for an optimum solution. If a problem-solver avoids the Reality Trough, he or she will miss opportunities to find complex solutions for complex problems.

When examining the implications of the individual's problems, there can be what most people consider to be negative feelings. Feelings such as shock, sadness, or possibly anger may surface as one realizes the extent of damage caused by the existing problems. The problem-solver needs to be able to accept these feelings, recognize their significance, bring them to the surface so reality is acknowledged. These emerging feelings are just a consequence of expanded awareness and a natural element of the costs of the status quo. The problem-solver should not avoid the surfacing of these feelings.

For most problems, the feelings will mostly be surprise at what the current situation actually costs. For some, the realization might be more dramatic as the individual discovers he or she has been ignoring substantial costs. The individual needs to be willing to let whatever is there rise to the surface of awareness. Through this insight, the individual will be more aware of the need to solve the problem and motivated to change.

An individual might feel the emotions of their situation more than a corporate representative because the individual is examining personal costs. However, these feelings can also be present in a corporate environment, particularly when a business manager, who is actually responsible for the area in which the problems exist, actually confronts costs they have simply accepted as a given. This type of exploration might surface awareness of a failure to manage as effectively as he or she should. This may lead to some expression of feelings of disappointment, anxiousness, or frustration.

Some problem-solvers wish to avoid these feelings, especially in situations where they are problem-solving with others. They're unsure how to respond when someone is visibly upset or experiencing a so-called negative emotional state. However, the more intensely the person with the problems examines these costs, and the more extensive they are, the higher the individual's motivation will be to find a solution to those problems.

Achieving constructive change will be so much easier when the problem-solver has moved through a deep Reality Trough. If an individual, couple, group or organization moves from awareness of the true costs and the real degree of pain to higher expectations, wanting better results and benefits, the problem-solver will be much more willing to make the change. The problem-solver acknowledges the need for a solution, and sooner rather than later.

Problem Solver's Responsibility

Shift From Disinterest, Resistance, Low Hope For Gain

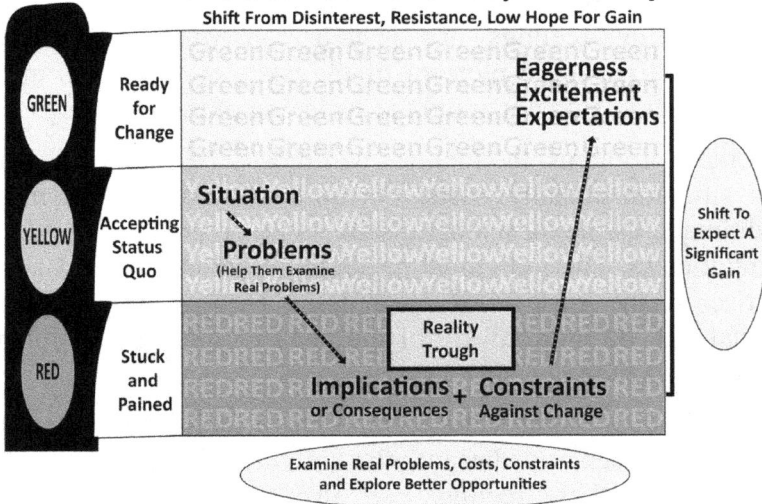

GREEN	Ready for Change	**Eagerness Excitement Expectations**
YELLOW	Accepting Status Quo	**Situation** → **Problems** (Help Them Examine Real Problems)
RED	Stuck and Pained	**Reality Trough** — **Implications** or Consequences + **Constraints** Against Change

Shift To Expect A Significant Gain

Examine Real Problems, Costs, Constraints and Explore Better Opportunities

Summary

People are more willing to undergo change, and are more enthusiastic about making change decisions when they can mentally organize what they discover about their own S.P.I.C.E[3]:

- their current situation,

- the problems they have in the current situation,

- the implications of those problems – what the problems or missed opportunities cost both tangibly and intangibly, how much frustration they cause, and the pain of the status quo,

- the constraints or reasons keeping the problem-solver from doing something about this before now, and

- their expectations about what a solution would have to do for them, their excitements about what they could gain if they effectively solve their problem(s), and their eagerness to get the problem solved.

Not only does this produce a readiness for change, but their S.P.I.C.E^3 becomes the definition of the problem to be solved.

Understand this process. See it as your responsibility to proceed through this S.P.I.C.E^3 cycle when you begin problem-solving. Explore your own S.P.I.C.E^3 to bring about new insights, and help yourself and others get ready for change. Then you will be able to find the proper solutions for your needs.

You will become a more effective person, couple, group or organization if you adopt a greater openness to change. Your success increases when you seek opportunities for growth and development, and engage in effective problem-solving to achieve new and better results. Problem-solving involves getting ready for change then engaging in creative processes and critical thinking in order to arrive at optimum solutions.

The Problem-Solving Sequence

Many people are quite random in how they solve their problems, and as a result, their outcomes are less than could be attained. It's extremely helpful to have, and follow, an organized problem-solving sequence. It works best if that sequence starts with a complete understanding of the problem to be solved – the S.P.I.C.E^3.

What you are about to read will likely challenge the assumptions and thoughts you may have about problem-solving. You will be confronted with a clearly organized approach, which contrasts sharply with how most people currently deal with their own difficulties or opportunities, and those they share with others.

Organized movement through the sequence of these steps will substantially increase the frequency of arriving at optimum solutions. This approach incorporates both unfettered creative thinking, and the more stringent critical thinking that leads to selection of an optimum solution and action. This approach has two halves, each with a different set of attitudes and thinking processes, plus a finishing step.

In the first half, the problem-solver is expected to set aside all judgement, evaluation, criticism and decision making. This is a fidgety time when the problem-solver's thinking and ideas bounce about in order to arrive at a problem definition and possible solutions. The focus is on expansive thinking, including all ideas and possibilities that both define the problem and could potentially bring about a solution.

The first half taps into the power of our subconscious, sometimes thought of as right brain activity. Much has been written about the link between creativity and subconscious thinking. The subconscious is the place of dreams, imagination, make-believe, shifts in perception, and acceptance of the impossible as possible. The first half in this problem-solving model capitalizes on the ability of the subconscious mind to suspend judgement and critical thinking, allowing us to entertain the fantastical, to consider the unusual as reasonable, to consider far-fetched ideas, to uncover "out-of-the box" options our conscious thinking just wouldn't allow us to consider.

This first half is a process of becoming unsettled, questioning the value of sticking with the status quo, opening up one's thinking that making the right change might bring about much better results. This half is about including as much information as possible in the formation of the problem definition, and including as many creative solution options as possible. The goal is to find new insights that lead to growth and development.

THE FIRST HALF – CREATIVE THINKING (FIDGET)

F	Feel The Need	Pay attention to any itch that suggests the current status quo is not fulfilling your needs and recognize any such deficit as a reason to engage in problem-solving.
I	Identify And Include Relevant Participants	Determine who is involved in the problem situation and invite them to engage in the problem-solving process.
D	Define The Problem	Sort through the S.P.I.C.E^3 of the problem-solver's situation.
G	Generate Solution Possibilities	Engage in a process which suspends all judgement, evaluation and criticism and produce as many solution possibilities as you can in a set time frame. Reach for the unexpected.
E	Elaborate	While continuing to suspend judgement, evaluation and criticism, elaborate each idea so that the idea is completely envisioned as a possible solution and clarify each idea to make sure that it is fully expressed and understood.
T	Take A Break	Take a break for five to ten minutes, twenty minutes to five hours, or one to five days depending on the severity and significance of the problem. Take this break to allow your subconscious to think about the work you've done so far. Respect any dreams, hunches, fantasies that emerge during the break period as more information to consider in your definition of the problem and elaboration of the ideas.

In the second half, the problem-solver is expected to shift into judgmental, critical, selective and decisive thinking, applying attitudes that favor selecting the best alternative. This critical thinking is associated with left brain activity where we work to take control over our world, form decisions, and make plans.

In this second half, the focus is not on inclusion but exclusion until the optimum solution stands on its own. The problem-solver works from many possibilities whittling down options until the best one has been identified and chosen. This is a stage of relaxing into implementation of the optimum solution(s).

THE SECOND HALF – CRITICAL THINKING (RELAX)

R	Review	Following the break, review the problem definition (the S.P.I.C.E^3) and the list of elaborated solutions, plus make changes if new information emerged during the break.
E	Evaluation	Critically assess the viability and actual benefits of each solution possibility. Measure the potential payoffs and costs as specifically as possible.
L	Lock Onto Your Optimum Solution(s)	Make a decision as to which solution possibility is the optimum solution for the problem, or in some cases, select a set of optimum solutions. This involves making a commitment to see that particular solution fully implemented.
A	Action Plan For Implementation	Make a very specific plan for implementation. Determine who is going to do what, where, when, how, and with what resources so that the selected solution is fully implemented.
X	eXecute	Follow the plan and implement the selected solution.

THE FINISH

Even though the problem has been solved (or not), problem-solving is not over. There is a finishing step.

A	Assess Results and Your Process	Determine if the desired results have been achieved and assess how effectively you engaged in problem-solving in this instance. If the desired results have not been achieved, engage in problem-solving again. From your analysis of your process, learn how to be more effective when working on the next problem or opportunity.

It's up to the problem-solver to organize his or her thinking, or the thinking of a couple or a group into these two halves, each with their own specific steps so that the most effective consideration of the problem and solution possibilities can take place. Once implementation has taken place, the problem-solver must then insure that the finishing step occurs with an intention to learn from this experience.

It helps to have this sequence as a map for how to proceed. You may wish to use a different map, language or organization for your own problem-solving behavior but you will have to successfully navigate through the steps in the process described here.

The First Half – FIDGET

Learn to use the energy within you that wants growth, wants challenge, desires creativity, wants to tackle issues, pursues learning and greater success. The acronym for this first half has been deliberately chosen to reflect this process of getting ready for change, of considering many other possibilities, of opening up one's mind to better ways of being.

Feel The Need

Include Relevant Participants

Define the Problem – Sort Out The S.P.I.C.E^3

Generate Solution Possibilities

Elaborate On Each Idea

Take A Break

Step One:
Feel The Need

Problem-solving requires some degree of recognition that there is a gap between where one is and where one could be or wants to be. That awareness can be terribly strong or simply a little itch that comes from your subconscious mind directing you to examine your status quo and question whether or not you can get better results than you're getting. Learn to pay attention to that itch.

Insight Potential When "Feeling The Need" – *The problem-solver may discover that the current status quo is not as comfortable as it once was, that he or she is not as happy with the status quo as first thought, that fresh desires for better results have emerged, that a growth has taken place in the problem-solver's aspirations, and change is needed. The problem-solver may recognize that his or her human tendency to deny the need for change is holding him or herself back; feel an itch to improve his or her results; and develop an expanded awareness of new opportunities for growth and development.*

The action to move from a current state of being to a new one is all about solving problems effectively and making effective change. However, problem-solving won't start until we feel the need to problem-solve, to make a change for better results. It's obvious that we must first feel the need.

We live in complex and changing environments. Our ability to adjust to our changing environment, to sustain some stability in that changing world, is a significant contributor to our success in life. This keeps us level and coordinated. Instead of reacting impulsively or reflexively to every change, we screen out many of the changes to maintain some manageability in our lives.

However, this also has the effect of reducing our personal performance over time if we don't truly adapt and change. Often old behaviors bring about diminished results in the new world. Or, new opportunities could present themselves where we might be able to achieve better results but our normal tendency might be to ignore them. Alternatively, if we hold a positive attitude toward problem-solving and pay attention to any diminished results or lost opportunities, we might develop a desire to bring about change.

Goals Of The Felt Need Stage

The first step is to know when to initiate problem-solving. Preferably, you will want to recognize the need before an issue has become a crisis. The earlier that you sense the need to initiate problem-solving behavior, the easier it will be to find a solution and the less costly the waiting period will be. To be an effective problem-solver, your goals would be to:

- Anticipate the need for, or opportunity for, positive changes that bring about greater success.

- Initiate problem-solving as early as possible.

- Discover new opportunities for improvement when your current situation is still in good shape.

- Commence problem-solving when you are in a calm and rational state as opposed to one of dire stress and emotional upheaval.

and

- Enter problem-solving as a fun-seeking adventure as opposed to one forced upon you because of a costly problem situation.

Feeling The Need

Problem-solving doesn't start until there is a felt need to close a gap between what one has and what one might prefer. There must be some sort of itch to make things better.

As problem-solvers, we differ in when and how we feel that itch. For some, the sense things are not the way they could be is pervasive. For such people, the world around them seems to ignore what is important. Such people are often seen as complainers, disgruntled and unhappy individuals. In contrast, there are people that see the world through rose-colored glasses and think what they have is wonderful and fully satisfying. Such people see no need for change. There are no gaps between what one has and what one wants. The rest of us fall somewhere between these two extremes.

There are times when we acknowledge a gap between what we have and what we want. From this acknowledgement, we might feel compelled to do something about the gap. There are also times when we deny that any gap exists, either ignoring any slight discomforts or accepting them as just the way things are. However, the degree to which we deny, to which we put up with any itch that tries to stir up a movement to a new state of being, limits our effectiveness as a problem-solver.

Within an individual, where an itch both exists and is ignored, this internal conflict will lead to tension. Whatever is precipitating the itch will likely go unsatisfied, and grow in intensity. This will progressively unsettle the problem-solver and demand attention.

In intimate relationships, if one spouse feels the need to bring about some sort of change but the other does not, then conflict arises. If one spouse feels the gap while the other says no gap (problem) exists, the couple is unable to enter into shared problem-solving. There will be tension in the relationship. The spouse that feels the need will be stymied, frustrated and unable to take cooperative action with the refusing spouse. This leads to one of three possibilities:

- persistent agitation within the spouse that feels the need,

- a shift to sharing the denial with the spouse that does not feel the need, thereby resulting in unmet needs and growing dissatisfaction, or

- individual problem-solving on the part of the spouse that has the felt need.

None of these three possibilities is healthy for the shared relationship, and is not an indication of effective problem-solving.

In work relationships, the same dynamic can prevail. If one member of a work group or team thinks there is a problem but others don't agree, frustrations will emerge. Again, the three possibilities prevail:

- persistent agitation within the group member that feels the need,

- a shift to sharing the denial with the rest of the group that does not feel the need, thereby allowing a possible problem to fester, or

- individual problem-solving on the part of the group member that has the felt need.

Again, none of these three possibilities is healthy for the shared relationship, and is not an indication of effective problem-solving. In turn, the unresolved problem will likely grow in size, or if the problem is tackled and solved by only one team member, the individually chosen solution is likely to become a new problem for the rest of the group.

If the small itch that a gap exists is ignored or denied, the problem is likely to grow in significance. If the gap grows between what one has and what one wants, the problem moves from a minor dissatisfaction to major frustration and eventually to a crisis. Ignored issues typically don't go away. They fester and become persistent sores.

Problem-solving is easier when the problems are small, more like new opportunities that can be pursued through creative engagement in problem-solving behavior. Problem-solving is much more stressful in crisis situations. Effectiveness improves when a person recognizes a need to engage in creative problem-solving at much earlier stages.

So the first step in effective problem-solving is the Felt Need step. The earlier that a problem-solver can feel the need to engage in effective problem-solving behavior, the easier the problem is to solve, and the problem-solving activity can be much more enjoyable.

Triggers

There are many different triggers that can bring about the feeling that a problem needs to be solved. These triggers will cause an itch to do something about the problem, and the problem-solver needs to pay attention and not just brush off that itch as inconsequential or treat it as only a minor irritation. Some of these triggers appear as:

DIMINISHING RETURNS

The problem-solver may experience diminishing results when using existing processes. Doing what has worked before might not work as well as it did. It's not going to work if the problem-solver just whips him or herself into trying harder at doing the same old stuff. The task would be to define what has caused the diminished results and find solutions to correct for this.

LESS EMOTIONAL REWARDS OVER TIME

In some cases, the problem is one of diminishing satisfaction with the feelings one has when doing things the same old way. For example, the individual, couple or group shifts from excitement with how things are to just satisfaction, and eventually to boredom with the repetition. The emotional rewards are no longer there.

INCREASED ERROR RATES

An increase in the number of errors and mistakes that are committed within your current processes can produce a feeling that a problem exists. To detect such problems, you need to measure your quality over time. Something has happened that has caused an increase in errors and that something needs to be discovered and the problem fully defined.

RISING STANDARDS

Alternatively, the problem might be the result of a desire to increase the standards for quality. If the problem-solver elects to demand better quality, then this change requires a change in processes or new solutions that would achieve this result. It would be a form of craziness to want better results while continuing to do the same old things.

CHANGES IN YOUR ENVIRONMENT

Things constantly change around us and that can make some aspects of the way we do things no longer relevant, less successful, or inappropriate given new opportunities. Environmental changes are probably the greatest impetus for the felt need to engage in problem-solving behavior.

INCREASED COMPETITION

More competitors may enter the environment and put downward pressures on the rewards the problem-solver is realizing from his or her current way of doing things, and upward pressures on the costs of doing what the problem-solver does. The incursion of others doing similar things or even things in a better way will put pressure on the problem-solver.

LOSS

Death, divorce, separation, being made obsolete by new technology, a reduction in control and power over a situation, business takeovers, floods, devastating storms or other catastrophes, aging and the loss of certain abilities are fall forms of loss that drive the immediate need to engage in problem-solving. Some problems or situations involve loss and grief for at least one or more people. When in a state of loss, it is easy to believe that the best that can be hoped for is to choose the least damaging of several tough options. Alternatively, such loss or grief can be used as a motivator to search out a much better outcome, results that exceed what one had before the loss. Within the despair of loss, such an achievement might initially be perceived as impossible. The challenge is to feel the itch to do something positive about the problem(s) the loss has caused.

NEW OPPORTUNITIES

The problem-solver may perceive new opportunities to achieve different and better results. New resources might come available. New offers that require a decision might be presented. Your internal awareness may be twitching with a felt need to examine your current situation to look for ways to achieve growth and development.

EXPANDED DESIRES

As we grow, we want more out of life. Our desires grow with us. This brings us face to face with new opportunities and problems. We might want to achieve new outcomes from what we do; or envy what others achieve; or wish to achieve something never before anticipated.

NEW PARTICIPANTS

One change that can produce the need to engage in problem-solving is the entrance of new participants. As others enter the situation, they bring their own needs and desires, preferences for how things are done, attitudes and beliefs that become part of the situation. This can create new gaps between the way things are and the way the participants want them to be.

AN INTUITIVE SENSE THAT THINGS COULD BE BETTER

Sometimes, we just have a slight sense that something isn't quite right, or that something could be better than it is. This might be experienced as feeling unsettled, less than satisfied, like something that you can't identify is missing. These feelings might just temporarily rise to the surface, but if ignored, will become more pervasive overtime.

Techniques For Feeling The Need

There are skills that can be used to enhance one's problem-solving effectiveness at this first step. The goal is pay greater attention to these triggers and to increase one's awareness of the need to close a gap. The earlier that a gap can be recognized, the better it is for achieving successful outcomes. Effective problem-solvers develop a repertoire of awareness expanding activities.

ANTICIPATE TRIGGERS

Most people think that one should fully enjoy the moment when everything is going well. It is great to fully experience accomplishment, satisfaction, joy when all is working effectively. However, the world will change.

One can wait until it has changed so much that the individual, couple or group has to change in response, or one can be a leader and anticipate how things might change, creating new opportunities and problem gaps. So, the greatest effectiveness comes from a combination of fully enjoying the present and taking moments to think about the following:

- What's coming in the way of change in our immediate environment?

- What about our current way of doing things could break down?

- What diminishing returns can we expect as other forces enter into our world (i.e. competition for the resources being used to do what we do; other participants; growth or development in existing participants; diminished demand for what we produce; etc.)

This does not mean dwelling on doom and gloom. This is a process of periodically assessing the current situation and asking if there are any threats to what you have. If so, you've generated a felt need to engage in effective problem-solving to bring about a new way of being that realizes new opportunities.

SCHEDULE TRIGGER SEARCHES

We all get busy in this dynamic world in which we live. We get into a rhythm of doing the same things over and over again because they've worked well for us. Your problem-solving effectiveness can be improved by simply scheduling in moments where you stop, assess, and ask yourself these questions:

- Am I getting the results I want?

- What might I want that I don't have right now?

- What might I have that I don't want right now?

- Am I experiencing greater pressure and working harder to get the results I'm getting?

- What things have changed around me that demand I make changes on my own part?

- Am I experiencing any frustration, disappointment, tension and if so, what is this about?

Periodically taking these reflective moments will allow you to stop and notice any itch you feel about the gap between what you have and what you want. Ignoring and denying the answers to these questions will only cause the discomfort to grow until you finally feel the need in a state of distress. Schedule in reflection as a part of your daily life and you will feel the need earlier.

OBTAIN FEEDBACK FROM OTHERS

You are used to looking at your world from your own perspective, and if things are going well, you see your life as the way you think it should be. One way to step out of your own view to discover new opportunities or to discover gaps within your own world is to ask others how they see you. What do they think might be missing elements of your growth and development? What opportunities do they think you're missing?

In personal life, turn to family and friends that know you well and care about you. Invite them to describe what they see as your current "state of the union" including what they see as your strengths, weaknesses, opportunities, and gaps, warts and all. You want their analysis of how you could improve so you can assess their feedback looking for new opportunities to problem-solve and grow.

If you're in a business or organizational context, you can do the same thing by hiring the services of a professional to do observation and analysis of your business and organizational processes, looking for areas where you could make improvement. By seeking an outsider's point of view, issues and opportunities may be perceived that you've taken for granted. If you aren't inclined to bring in outsiders to do this, set up internal processes where members of the organization can comment on what they think are problems, areas needing improvement, and new opportunities.

Whether an individual, couple or group, assess what you learn from the feedback you receive and look for new "felt needs" to engage in effective and creative problem-solving. Let others help you to stretch your boundaries and grow.

ASSESS YOUR SHARED STATE OF THE UNION

Similar to seeking the impressions of others, schedule a meeting with significant others expressly for the purpose of asking each other, "Are there any concerns with <u>our</u> current state of the union that could be discussed." If everything is going well, these concerns could be minor irritations, niggling feelings that something is missing, or a bit of interest or excitement about something new that has emerged in the world.

By gathering together as a ritual to look for new opportunities when things are going very well, you open the door to problem-solving before you have to deal with festering issues. This type of problem-solving is fun, an adventure looking for ways to enrich what you already have, a form of taking over more control of the changes in your shared life or work. Create a change ready culture within your relationship, group or organization.

ASK "WHAT IF"

Everything is sweet. You're happy, contented, pleased with your accomplishments. The tendency would be to just enjoy what you have, pressing on as if it will continue indefinitely. Alternatively, you could periodically stop and ask yourself, "What if this stops or breaks down and I no longer have....?"

The goal isn't to lead you into depression and anxiety over losing the good life. The goal is to consider what might change, because change is inevitable, and then engage in effective and creative problem-solving to develop strategies to deal with any such changes before they happen. Just as survivalists store food, emergency equipment and safety supplies when they are readily available in case some future catastrophe occurs, you act like a survivalist, develop a new felt need and prepare for the "what if's" you can predict.

THINK ABOUT A PERFECT WORLD

No matter how well things are going for you, there are likely opportunities for things to be better. Stop periodically and think about how things could be even grander. What more could you achieve? What could you do that you haven't yet done? How could things be done more efficiently or effectively? Who could you share your world with that you aren't yet connected with? Where could you be that you haven't been?

Just ask yourself, "If everything could be perfect, what would I have that I don't have now?" Create the felt need as you imagine new areas for improvement, growth, change. Use your ability to dream big to identify new opportunities.

PRETEND YOU'RE SOMEONE ELSE

One way to open up your own sense of how things could be better for you than they currently are is to identify someone that you particularly admire. Perhaps you could think of someone who has something you want, or pick a famous person that you hold in high esteem. Imagine yourself as this person, but then imagine that person living as you are now. Think about the felt needs that person would have given their drive to be him or herself. Something would need to be different for this person so they could be the person you admire.

This technique can be used in a business situation. Your business is working well, there are no immediate issues that cause you to feel a felt need to engage in problem-solving. So pick a business that you admire – it can be a competitor, or some business from a completely different industry. Then pretend to be that business but imagine them "trapped" in your business. What would that business feel as a felt need to bring about change to achieve what they need or want.

IMAGINE EVERYTHING FAILS – START OVER

You've got it all. Life is good. You have no felt need for things to be different. There are no gaps between what you have and what you want. So imagine that it all falls apart.

You're Tom Hanks in *Castaway* and your plane goes down, stranding you on a mid-ocean unpopulated island. Your employment, relationships, possessions are all taken away. Now start over and imagine what you need or want within a completely changed world.

In such a fantasy, the gaps between what you have and what you want will be plentiful and huge. Pick the ones that most excite you and use them as motivators to engage in effective and creative problem-solving.

Some people think this is unnecessary doomsday thinking. Yes, it is negative thinking in the midst of your real life going well, but it is done with a significant purpose. Even though you think life is currently swell, you can take a break, put your feet up, lean back and engage in fantasy that will not destroy what you have.

You are simply stimulating your mind to consider potential growth, desired changes, new opportunities. You don't have to actually make the changes but you can entertain the possibilities with no harm.

BREATHE

When in a situation where you feel intense feelings of haste, or concern that you just don't have enough time, stop and take a series of four deep breathes, relaxing with each exhale. Allow your subconscious mind to offer up any signals that all is not well and problem-solving is required. By pausing, relaxing, you have an opportunity to feel any prevailing triggers and recognize the need to engage in problem-solving behavior.

However, in some cases, you might find yourself in an emergency situation where an immediate decision must be made, an immediate action must be taken. In such cases, you can feel the need but it might feel like there is no time to stop and consciously follow the full set of problem-solving steps.

It may be that you have to open a mental doorway for your subconscious mind to quickly offer up a suggestion for what you should do. As a result of evolution, the human brain has been shaped by survival during millions of fight or flight moments that required an instantaneous response. The oldest part of the technology within our brain can process everything perceived through our senses and make an instantaneous decision in such moments. So, after feeling the need, just stop and take a series of deep breaths. Look around your situation. Don't force anything but attend to whatever emerges in your thoughts.

Allow your subconscious to offer up a way to react to the situation. Each deep breath keeps you from reflexively reacting in the wrong way. Quickly assess the risks of doing what your subconscious has offered up, and if it looks like the right thing to do, take it. If you share the emergency with others, you could ask them all to stop, take a breath, and to listen to whatever thoughts emerge in their thinking. Then get everyone to share what popped up. This might give some other options or actually provide some consensus.

Conversely, in some other situations, the felt need might revolve around a rather small issue or problem. Often insignificant problems don't require long drawn out problem-solving. If you have a feeling that something small needs to be fixed right now or that you need to make a minor decision, then you can do the same. Just stop, take a deep breath, quiet yourself, look around the situation, and allow your thoughts to emerge. You may find that your subconscious offers up a quick and acceptable solution.

This is the "Blink" phenomenon that Malcolm Gladwell wrote about in *Blink: The Power of Thinking Without Thinking*, (Penguin Books Ltd, 2006). By taking these deep breathes and allowing the subconscious to offer up a solution, we take a short cut and make a decision without consciously proceeding through an extensive problem-solving process.

However, our skill at doing this primarily grows through significant prior problem-solving experiences. The expertise we develop over time allows our subconscious mind to size up the situation, find similarities and strategies that worked in the past, and make a quick choice for what is right in this situation.

In most cases, the problem will be neither a large emergency or a small inconsequential issue, and taking the deep breaths will allow you to attend to any trigger that produces the feeling that you should stop and deal with the problem effectively. In doing so, you can schedule in a problem-solving session to resolve the concern.

Improved Personal Performance

By using techniques such as this to expand your feeling that there is a need to problem-solve, you increase your chances that you will arrive at new insights. Such insights enhance your personal performance. You will lead yourself to have them while others may not, so this also enhances your competitive standing relative to others that are more complacent about change. Knowing that it's time to engage in problem-solving to bring about effective personal change gives you both a greater chance at effective management of what the world throws at you, and an advantage over others.

You don't have to use any of these particular skills. You can choose to simply work on greater awareness of your own felt need by paying attention when you have frustrations, irritations, unfulfilled desires, niggling wants, fantasies. However, we all tend to get so busy that we don't pay attention all that well.

Too often, these ignored, small, early little itches have to fester, grow and become screaming pains before we stop and give them attention. As a result, we're often problem-solving in situations of difficulty or crisis. Be a more effective problem-solver by developing strategies to face new opportunities before they become monster issues.

When To Move To The Next Step

It's time to move to the next step when you've brought your awareness around to an acknowledgement that there may be a gap between the way things are and the way they could be. You're ready for the next step when you've acknowledged that itch.

If the problem-solver is a group or a couple, then each individual may experience the felt need in a different manner. Some may not even feel that a problem exists. It is not productive to make the person or persons who think there is a problem defensively argue their case in front of a wall of others who are contented with the status quo.

It is more effective to simply agree that if one person thinks there is a need to engage in problem-solving, it is appropriate to move to the next step, where you will include all participants that might have a stake in the problem, and then collectively flesh out what the problem might be.

> In simple terms, if one person feels the need, the need exists. So move to the next step.

Using the process described in this book, this can be done relatively quickly. Once the next two steps are done, the existence of the problem will be established, or not, in the minds of all participants. This will happen easier if those who do not yet feel the need set aside all of their resistance and cooperatively engage in fleshing out the problem definition.

Transition To The Next Step

Recognizing that you feel the need to problem-solve, you need to make a transition to the next step. The transition is as simple as thinking to yourself,

> "Okay, I think there is a gap between what I have and what I want. So who else is involved in this?"

or saying to others that also feel the need,

> "Given that we think there is a gap between what we have now and what we want, we need to involve anyone else that might feel the same way. So who should we approach?"

Step Two:
Include Relevant Participants

A problem-solver can be one person, a couple, a small group, or a larger community. Whoever is involved in the problem situation has a stake in whatever change is brought about through any problem-solving effort. If a relevant person is excluded, then that person is highly likely to resist any change that some other problem-solver brings about. Problem-solving effectiveness is highest when the right people are involved, and when the people involved fully commit to the solution that will be used to solve the problem. There are techniques that can be used to include multiple people in the problem-solving process.

Insight Potential When "Including Relevant Participants" – *The problem-solver might be surprised by discovering someone who should be included that wasn't initially considered to be a relevant participant. The problem-solver, through discussion with relevant others, may realize that there is more to the problem than first considered and develop a better appreciation for what others see as the problem and most appropriate solution.*

There may be problems that affect only the problem-solver, and in those instances, the person feeling the need to problem-solve can proceed to look for a new optimum solution on his or her own. However, it is likely that there are significant others that reside in the problem-solver's status quo.

John Donne wisely wrote, " No man is an island entire of itself; every man is a piece of the continent, a part of the main." An individual seldom has a problem that does not involve others, a problem that is exclusively his or hers alone. If we solve a problem and bring about change, that change is likely to impact significant others. It works best if those significant others are included in the problem-solving process so that they can share in bringing about a change that works for them as well.

Once one person feels the need to problem-solve, then that person must think about who else is relevant to the problem. This person or these persons should be included in any problem-solving efforts because their input will be critical to finding a solution that works. By including these significant others, the problem can be more fully defined, a broader range of solution possibilities can be considered, and there is a much higher likelihood that an optimum solution will be found and implemented effectively.

Goals Of This Step

As simple and brief as this step is, there are several accomplishments to pursue in completing step two.

- Whenever possible, include every person that shares the problem.

- Include every person that will ultimately participate in making any decision about what change(s) to make.

- Identify and include any significant person or group that is going to be impacted by any potential change when a new solution is implemented.

- Expand your problem-solving resources by including the knowledge and expertise of others.

- Treat your own felt need as part of a larger world view that others may, or may not, share.

- Open up your own mind to the potentially larger scope of the problem as you include other points of view.

and

- Create a problem-solving culture in your own mind, amongst your significant others, and within your shared community.

Techniques For Step Two

You can do various things to add to your effectiveness at Step Two. Certainly, the simplest approach is to just ask yourself, "Who else is part of this problem?" and "Who else would care about anything I might do to bring about change and improvement?" However, there are a few techniques that you could alternatively use to make sure the right people are included and your understanding of the problem is expanded.

PRETEND THERE IS AT LEAST ONE OTHER

If you try to identify others that might share your concerns or similarly believe that an opportunity to engage in problem-solving exists, and can't think of anyone, then make up a fictional other. This may seem to take you to the edge of being crazy but it can help. It just takes a bit of make believe on your part.

Just as Tom Hanks, playing the role of a stranded Chuck Noland in Castaway, paints a face on a volleyball that drifted up to shore and names it Wilson, and then talks to it as he solves his survival problems, you can make up your own character and talk to it. Hanks gave Wilson a point of view in every problem, as if Wilson talked back to him, and you can do the same. You too can talk to your fictional other as if he or she is present and let your subconscious put words into his or her mouth to answer you back.

PRESENT YOUR CONCERN

If you think the problem situation might involve only one or two others such as a spouse or family members, or yourself and your boss or close work colleagues, then ask for a meeting where you can sit with the other people and describe this feeling you have that there is a need or opportunity to engage in problem-solving. Do this with humility and a tentative attitude, as opposed to any flaming excitement and insistence that there is a problem.

Suggest that now would be a good time to examine your status quo and consider opportunities for bringing about improvement and enhanced results. Make it clear that you don't see the other person as a problem but as a party that has a vested interest in any problem-solving that might occur. Explain that you think his or her input is critical to finding an optimum solution.

Share your own awareness that a gap might exist between the way things are and the way things could be. Indicate you would like to examine that gap and determine if it makes sense to engage in problem-solving to close the gap.

Ask for thirty minutes to sit together to discuss your shared S.P.I.C.E.[3]. This will likely require that you first explain the concept of S.P.I.C.E.[3] and how this is a particularly helpful way to define a problem, if one exists. Explain that you would like to talk with him or her about:

- the situation you share,

- any symptoms and problems that might reside within that context,

- the implications of those problems in terms of tangible and intangible costs,

- the constraints that have kept the situation from changing for the better before now, and

- the expectations and excitements that each of you might have about what could be achieved if change brings about better results.

Indicate that you haven't yet done this on your own and would highly appreciate the other person's insights.

ASK IF OTHERS HAVE ANY CONCERNS

Instead of telling your significant others that you think a problem exists, you could approach each of them and indicate you want to know how each of them feels about how things are going. Indicate you would like to make this a regular ritual – a temperature check of sorts where you want to find out if people are satisfied with the status quo, or if they have any concerns about how things are, or if they are feeling an itch to pursue any new opportunities.

Use active listening skills (invitations, inference checks, paraphrases, feelings checks, identification, explained questions – See Appendix 2) to draw out the thoughts, feelings and desires of each of these significant others. Make sure you understand each person's point of view and that he or she knows you understand. The other person must believe that you wanted his or her input and not just an opportunity to tell him or her what you think, feel, desire. The other person shouldn't feel ambushed. Once you have this understanding, you could ask if the other person wants to hear what you have to offer and then share your own thoughts, feelings and desires.

There is a risk to this technique. If you approach asking questions of the other person before you share your own thoughts, he or she can wonder what you have as a hidden agenda. However, once you share your own thoughts, feelings and desires, you may have already colored the other person's thinking. So you have several options:

- Describe your own itch in general terms first, then ask if the other person has any of his or her own. Indicate that your own growing awareness suggests that new opportunities for improved results might exist and ask if the other person shares any of that thinking.

- Do your best to see the world the way the other person might see it, then approach him or her and use the skill of identification to describe how you imagine the other person experiences the current situation and guess at thoughts, feelings, desires he or she might have to make it better.

- Get each person to write down his or her own thoughts, feelings and desires privately, write out your own, then throw the written ideas into a pile and read them one at a time.

PICK YOUR TEAM

Make a list of all the people somehow involved in your status quo. List each of the people you can think of even if they are only tangentially involved. Once you have a full list, consider each person's relative importance to the itch that you feel. Who is most centrally involved in your situation and might have thoughts, feelings and desires related to the belief you have that some problem-solving needs to be undertaken? Invite them to join you in problem-solving around that itch.

If this is a situation that involves more than one or two of you, pick a team. If there is a small group, include all of them but try to keep the group around five people. If there are a few people that you think represent the same possible input or concerns, then pick the person that you think would best represent that point of view to include in this group. On the other hand, if your list includes a great many people, consider involving all of them in a community problem-solving session using the Nominal Group Technique which is described later in this book.

CONDUCT A SURVEY

Start from your own feeling that things are not as you want them to be and devise a questionnaire that you can present to others who in some way are potentially related to your area of concern. Make this five to ten questions so the questionnaire is easy to quickly fill out.

In the introduction to the survey, tell your potential survey participants that you want to assess their levels of satisfaction with regard to a specific aspect of the status quo that you share. Don't suggest that a problem exists but that you want to get a quick measure of everyone's level of satisfaction.

Emphasize that you want to know their specific thoughts and feelings so that you can follow-up with them if any further discussion is required. Tell each of them you are looking for input from all of the people involved, and ask each person to take a few minutes to complete your survey.

If you are conducting the survey by mail, indicate you've enclosed an addressed envelope complete with postage. Indicate that filling out the survey and putting it in the envelope will take approximately eight minutes of their time. Although an arbitrary number, I think eight minutes is the maximum amount of time it should take to fill out such a questionnaire.

Your survey should fit on one side of an 8½" by 11" page and should contain no more than ten questions. Explain how the questions in the survey work. You could try a mix of different types of questions or one question type. Use questions you think will get you information useful to you.

For example, you might have ten questions where you ask your respondent to rate their satisfaction on a five point scale from 1 = very low to 5 = very high, or to rate how well things are going in the status quo on a five point scale where 1 = very poorly to 5 = very well. Or you might have ten statements where you ask your respondent to indicate agreement with each statement on a ten point scale from 1 = strongly disagree to 10 = strongly agree.

You could use open-ended questions that require the respondent to write his or her response on the survey form. This requires more work on your respondent's part, and may cause your response rate to drop, but you might get useful comments from the hand-written additions. If using open-ended questions, have fewer of them.

The particular aspect of your status quo that triggers your need to engage in problem-solving will determine what you should ask in your questions. For example, a wife and mother might have feelings of disappointment about how the household is being maintained while she is working full time. A survey of the family members could involve a few questions such as:

- How satisfied are you right now with how the household looks, feels, works?

- How satisfied are you with the time we spend together in family activities having fun, exploring new things, getting out of the house together?

- How comfortable are you bringing your friends and colleagues to our house?

- How much do you agree with the statement that *the work each of us is doing to maintain our household is equally shared and fairly distributed*?

- How much do you agree with the statement that *a house only needs as much work as it takes to keep it reasonably tidy and organized*?

In another example, a person in a work group might have feelings that the group's work project might be proceeding in the wrong direction. A survey of group members could involve a few questions such as:

- How satisfied are you right now that our project is proceeding effectively?

- How much do you agree with the statement that *each of us has had a chance to contribute our own ideas and input to this project and feels fully valued as a project group member*?

- How comfortable are you that we will achieve the best possible outcome with this project?

- If you imagine how others might evaluate our work, how satisfied do you think they are with our progress so far?

In general, you want to ask questions that cause the respondent to examine their own thinking, their own itches for something better, their own feeling that it would be a good thing to engage in problem-solving. For rating scale questions, you could use some of the following:

- How comfortable do you feel with how things are in our current situation?

- How well do we do what we do?

- To what degree do you have any concerns in our current situation?

- How well do we use our time when we .... ?

- Thinking about the results that we currently achieve, how satisfied are you that we are doing as well as we could?

Alternatively, you could ask questions seeking a simple Yes/No/Maybe response plus handwritten responses on two blank lines under each rating. For example, you could ask:

Do you feel like anything is missing in our current situation?

Yes   No   Maybe – Please explain:

_____

_____

Using this format, you could ask other questions such as:

- Do you think you're getting enough rewards from the effort you expend in our current situation?

- Do we have enough knowledge and expertise to gain greater success?

- Do you see any opportunities to achieve better results than we currently get?

- Do you feel any discomfort with how we currently do what we do?

- Does any part of you have a desire for change and improvement, or consideration of new opportunities?

It's your survey questionnaire, so design it so it works for you. Prepare a survey with questions that fit your need to find out if any of the significant others has any felt need to engage in problem-solving.

* * *

By using these techniques to invite others to join you in problem-solving for improvement, your efforts will likely cause others to feel the need to problem-solve earlier than they might have on their own. In addition, you will be contributing to the creation of a problem-solving culture. A problem-solving culture is one that is characterized by:

- a continuous pursuit of improvement,

- a willingness to set aside current satisfaction to consider whether or not anything can be improved,

- an openness to the notion that if one person thinks something is in need of improvement, it is important to consider that possibility,

- a greater readiness to engage in problem-solving, and

- frequent improvements in the results that are achieved.

When To Move To The Next Step

In this step, you determined who else should be involved in any efforts to bring about change and improvement, and then stimulated each person to feel the need to engage in problem-solving. Once you've included the right group of problem-solving participants, or once you're satisfied that you are the only person that shares this concern, then move to Step Three and define the problem.

Transition To Step Three

If the problem-solver is an individual, he or she should review just exactly how to work on this problem. When working alone, commit to a sequential, step-by-step problem-solving process. I recommend that you either use the one contained in this book, or make sure that your own has all of the elements of this one.

If the problem-solver is a couple or group, then the group must decide together what steps to follow to solve this problem. If all couple or group members have not previously agreed on a sequential problem-solving process, the group is highly likely to flip flop around the steps. This produces group conflict, frustration, and dissatisfaction with the results of such meetings.

By agreeing in advance to the problem-solving process, the couple or group can approximate an organized progression through the steps and perform much better. This process brings about much better results, engages the group members more thoroughly, and leaves a greater satisfaction with participation in the creative process. One of the members must say something like:

> "Before we move forward on this problem, we need to discuss and decide what steps we will follow in the problem-solving process."

Once a commitment has been made by all to follow a particular process, shift to defining the problem. This will entail sorting out the problem-solver's S.P.I.C.E^3. If the problem-solver is a single person, then he or she should make a personal commitment to sort out all that is known about his or her S.P.I.C.E^3 as the next step.

"Okay, it's time to define my problem (my S.P.I.C.E^3) and record all that I know about this problem."

If the problem-solver is two or more people, then the person who invited others to work on the problem should explain the concept of S.P.I.C.E^3 as a problem definition. The participants must first arrive at a shared understanding of the S.P.I.C.E^3 in this situation.

"Okay, we're in this together. It's now time to define the problem and I propose that we do this by writing out everything we know about the situation, the problems within it, the costs of those problems, any constraints that we think inhibit progress, and what we would like to achieve as better results. If we do this, we will all better understand what we are dealing with here – our shared S.P.I.C.E^3. Are you all okay with this approach?"

Get materials together that can be used to write and organize the information as it surfaces. This could involve a writing pad, a flip chart and paper, a computer with word processing software attached to a projector, or a tablet. Once the recording media are available, begin to talk about the current situation (the S in S.P.I.C.E^3).

Step Three:
Define The Problem
(Sort Out The S.P.I.C.E^3)

There are many key elements to a full problem definition. Clearly examining those elements before looking for a solution is critical to finding the right solution(s). The problem-solver, whether individual, couple, group, or community will perform better and have a better chance of achieving optimum results if the problem is fully defined and commonly understood.

Insight Potential When "Defining The Problem" – The problem-solver may realize that there is more to the problem than first considered; may develop a better appreciation of the current resources in the situation that can help resolve the problem; may discover what failing to solve the problem is truly costing; might recognize that particular constraints prevent some possible solutions; could potentially acknowledge that some constraints are not real impediments and can be easily dealt with; might form new higher order goals and desires; and may form greater urgency to find a solution. If more than one person is involved, the problem-solver may understand the problem in new ways after hearing what others have offered as their perception of the issue(s).

After developing your awareness that there may be a gap between where you are now and where you want to be, and after inviting relevant others to join you in problem-solving, it's time to engage in the next step of effective and creative problem-solving. Move from a weak sense that something could be better to a full and organized description of the problem(s).

Goal Of The Problem Definition Step

This is a critical step in the problem-solving sequence and should probably take up half the time you intend to spend on your problem-solving effort. This is because there are many ways to underestimate the nature of the problem, to fail to see resources lying in plain sight within the problem situation, and to set the bar too low for the goals that the problem-solver wants to achieve.

Instead, take time to fully define the problem and make sure there is full clarity for what it is that the problem-solver wants to solve.

- Get a clear understanding of where you are now and where you want to be so the gap is fully understood.

- Develop a comprehensive understanding of the S.P.I.C.E^3 in this problem situation:

  ➢ expand awareness of the resources that reside within the situation for potential use as a solution,

  ➢ identify and understand any symptoms and difficulties in the current situation that indicate there is a problem and clarify the cause of the problem so you are working to solve the right issue(s),

  ➢ explore all of the costs, both tangible and intangible, of these symptoms and problems,

  ➢ clarify all of the forces, roadblocks, and constraints that keep you where you are and away from where you want to be,

  ➢ develop clarity about the minimal expectations that must be satisfied by a solution,

❯ identify highly desirable results that create excitement, and

❯ determine the deadline by which the problem must be solved.

plus

• Build a sense of purpose and excitement about what could be accomplished if the optimum solution can be identified.

Get The S.P.I.C.E^3

If a problem is the gap between where we are now and where we want to be, then a definition of the problem should show that gap between the status quo and our goal, and the deadline by which we would like to achieve our goal.

An effective problem definition requires a full understanding of the situation as it is now, a clarification of all the symptoms and deficiencies that indicate a problem exists, the costs and implications of these problems, the constraints that impede movement from where you are now, the minimum expectations you might have for what you want to achieve, the exciting results or benefits you really would like to achieve, and the eagerness you have to get the desired outcomes.

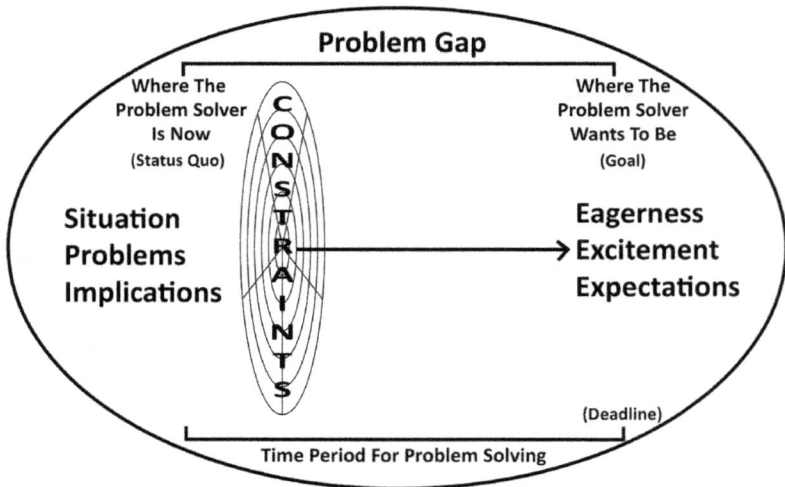

Problem Gap

Where The Problem Solver Is Now (Status Quo)

Where The Problem Solver Wants To Be (Goal)

CONSTRAINTS

Situation
Problems
Implications

Eagerness
Excitement
Expectations

(Deadline)

Time Period For Problem Solving

Each of the five main elements to a full definition of a problem contains important information.

Situation	the current situation, what one does, what is currently used to do what one does, how one does what one does, when one does it, where one does it, why one does it, who is the doer, and resources in the situation that aren't typically used.
Problems	the symptoms, deficiencies, difficulties, real problems, challenges, friction, and the tension one has when doing what one does; and any opportunities and wishes one has to do it better.
Implications	what the problem costs both tangibly and intangibly, when one isn't able to do what one wants to do as well as one would like; and the feelings one has about these costs, including feelings about lost opportunities.
Constraints	why one hasn't fixed this problem or concern before now; what has blocked one from taking appropriate action; and how one feels about these blockages.
E^{3}xpectations/ excitements/eager-ness	the goal or goals; what one would minimally expect to gain; what results would be really exciting (reduced costs, increased profit/gain, new opportunities, better results and benefits); and how eager one is to get the problem solved.

The objective in defining the problem in this way is to develop new insights about the problem-solver's S.P.I.C.E^3. As these insights accumulate, the problem-solver will be working on the right problem. If more than one person is involved, it is paramount that the participants all share an understanding of the problem so they can work together and in the same direction toward a solution.

The iceberg analogy applies to understanding the full extent of the problem. Only about 30% of an iceberg is visible above water, while the rest is hard to discern below the water line and almost invisible. The same is true about any problem we might have. Only a small portion of the problem is initially known to the problem-solver while a much larger portion is unknown or below awareness. The hidden portion is buried within our subconscious mind and needs to be extracted. The objective is to bring all of this hidden information forward into conscious awareness.

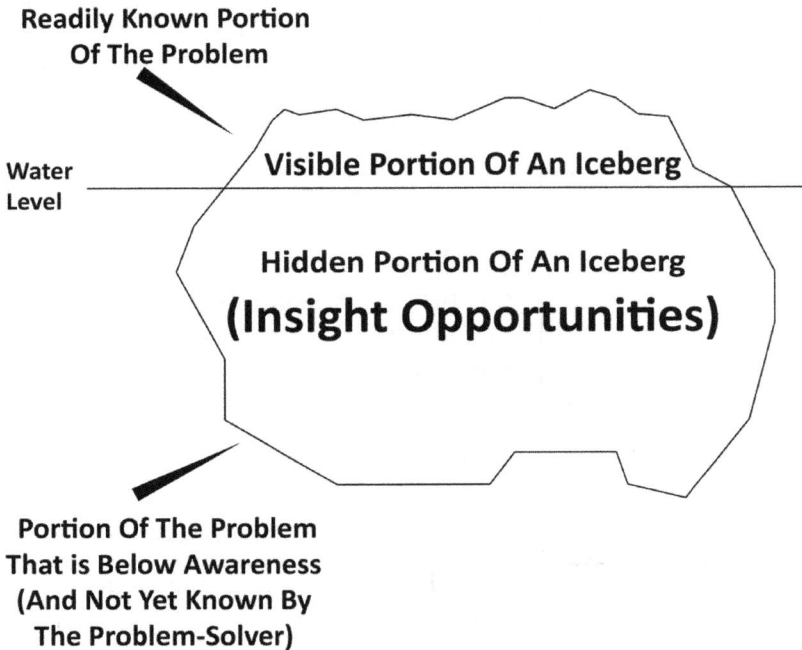

**Readily Known Portion
Of The Problem**

**Water
Level**

Visible Portion Of An Iceberg

Hidden Portion Of An Iceberg
(Insight Opportunities)

**Portion Of The Problem
That is Below Awareness
(And Not Yet Known By
The Problem-Solver)**

Working through the S.P.I.C.E^3 expands the problem-solver's understanding of what he or she is dealing with and takes the problem-solver to a readiness for change. By sorting through all of the elements of S.P.I.C.E^3, the problem-solver is nudged from the comfort of the status quo to a discovery of his or her real problem, into the Reality Trough where the problem-solver realizes how much the status quo actually costs. After spending half of the time available for problem-solving to fully develop clarity about the S.P.I.C.E^3, the problem-solver should wind up feeling a great deal of excitement about desirable new benefits that could be achieved if an optimum solution is identified (the goal).

A problem-solver must endeavor to discover as much about the problem as possible before seeking a solution. Questions must be asked about each of the five S.P.I.C.E[3] elements to expand awareness and determine the real problem. The following sample questions could be asked to uncover each of the five elements. Even if the felt need was triggered by frustration over certain problematic symptoms, you would generally first focus on a clarification of the current situation.

Situation Questions – These questions help you gather data and facts about the status quo to help you better know your situation, the people involved, and the resources within it.

- What is it we do in our current situation?
- Why do we do this?
- How do we do what we do now?
- What resources do we use?
- Are there any other resources in our current situation that currently are underutilized or go unused?
- Who does what we do?
- When do we do what we do?
- Who is influenced by what we do?
- Where do we do what we do – what is that environment like?
- What benefits do we currently realize from doing what we do?

Situation Insight Potential - reframing the problem-solver's perception of his or her own situation so he or she can see, hear, feel, understand the situation differently; discovering previously undervalued resources within the current situation that might be useful when a new solution is identified; clarifying further who is involved; and liberating an ability to consider new possibilities.

The goal is to broaden the problem-solver's awareness of what the situation is, because within the current situation, there are likely to be unused resources and key parties that will influence problem-solving success. Part of focusing on the situation first is learning what the problem-solver is doing well. It will make it easier for the problem-solver to then consider what isn't being done so well and the nature of his or her problems.

As you expand your awareness of your current situation, you may begin to think about the problem(s) within your status quo. If awareness of the problems does not emerge on its own, then ask one of the problem questions to direct your attention there.

Problem Questions – You ask these questions to uncover the symptoms, deficiencies, difficulties, dissatisfactions, real problems, challenges, hopes and opportunities you have in your current situation. This will likely lead you to see and understand your problem(s) differently, realize you have problems you hadn't recognized before, and see new opportunities not yet considered.

- What gaps are there between what we want and what we have?
- What about the current situation is irritating, frustrating, causing tension?
- What do we think are the symptoms that indicate we have a problem?
- What is the frequency of these symptoms?
- What do we think causes these symptoms or dissatisfactions in our current situation?
- What don't we like about the results we realize from our current way of doing things?
- When did we first start to think that our results aren't as good as we think could be achieved?
- If we were to say our current way of doing things could be improved, what would we improve?
- What in our current environment causes us to adjust what we do in order to get our things done?

> **Problem Insight Potential** - converting what you previously assumed to be just normal attributes of the current situation into perceived symptoms of a problem that needs to be resolved and not just accepted; exposing the real problem when that problem has not previously been understood; discovering the underlying causes of the symptoms; determining the extent of the gap between the way things are and the way we want them to be; uncovering any opportunities for improvement.

As the problem-solver discovers and clarifies problems, he or she might also get clues as to the consequences of these problems. There is significant insight potential when a problem-solver considers what the status quo truly costs. This is a critical point in problem-solving. If the problem-solver hasn't yet explored the implications, he or she will have to ask implication-oriented questions.

Implication Questions – These questions determine the consequences of the problems, specifically by discovering the degree of quantifiable cost, frustration, and pain the problem-solver has within his or her status quo.

- What are the costs of these symptoms, difficulties, and problems?

- Are we encountering any unanticipated costs because of our problems?

- If things aren't working as well as we would like, what does it cost to stick with the status quo?

- Are there any particular costs that would result from delaying the solution to this problem?

- Are there any tangible costs in continuing with our current set-up such as maintenance costs, downtime and wasted manpower, personnel turnover?

- Are there any intangible costs, such as morale issues, quality being less than we would like, emotional costs such as disappointment or frustration?

- Are there any hidden costs doing things the way we do them now?

- Has this problem held us back in any way from achieving our goals and targets?

- Are we experiencing any of the following costs:

  ➢ costs of error or failure,

  ➢ downtime costs,

  ➢ maintenance costs,

  ➢ lost opportunities,

  ➢ negative impact on the people involved,

  ➢ costs of delay in fulfilling the needs of others.

The problem-solver needs to learn both the tangible and intangible costs of the way things are now. Ideally, he or she should know the financial implications – the dollar costs the problem-solver has now. Quantify costs as much as possible but also notice the emotions that you have about these costs.

By taking stock, the problem-solver will see how much not solving the problem will continue to cost him or her. The problem-solver's motivation to find a solution will rise if he or she concludes that these costs are no longer acceptable.

> **Implication Insight Potential** – by facing what has previously been unconsciously denied, the problem-solver will likely discover the full costs of the problems, suddenly realizing that the consequences of not taking action are too great to live with or accept any longer.

The process of defining the problem(s) might now slow down because the problem-solver bumps up against what is stopping him or her from solving the problem(s). Or the problem-solver might hear him or herself state something like "But, there isn't much we can do about this." The problem-solver now needs to focus on what is preventing a solution. Get at this with a constraint-focused question.

Constraint Questions – Constraints are often the excuses that you've used to explain why you haven't made a change before now. Questions are asked to uncover what you see as roadblocks and then to find out which are real constraints and which are imagined. Ask and answer a few of these questions to clarify what you believe is keeping you locked into your own status quo.

- What excuses are used to justify why you are in the situation you're in?

- Have there been any particular reasons why you haven't made a change before now?

- Are there any real roadblocks preventing you from making improvements?

- Are there any limitations to our resources that will limit the size of the solution we could consider (limited finances, only a few people available to do the work, small spaces, deadlines)?

- What alternatives have already been tried or considered, and what prevented them from producing your desired outcomes?

- What roadblocks would an effective solution have to overcome?

- What resistance to change might you or others have?

Constraints can be financial, rule based, physical capability, environmental limitations, attitudes, lack of skills, contractual obligations, strategic, scheduling requirements, beliefs and values, a low level of willingness to undergo change on the part of the problem-solver, or alternatively, the problem-solver might think others are unwilling to take the risks of change. The points of view of a significant decision-maker might represent a possible constraint and this should be identified and addressed here.

Part of the exploration of constraints would include a determination as to the reality of these constraints. Are they real or imagined? Ask further questions like one of the following:

- Of the roadblocks you've identified, which ones most significantly get in your way?

- Sometimes people think a constraint prevents taking action, but when they really examine the constraint, they realize it's something they can work around. Does this apply to any that you've just listed?

- If you prioritize the constraints in terms of their importance, whicht constraints would be the most important and which constraints are less limiting?

- There are times when people limit their own ability to make changes. Thinking about the constraints you've identified, are any of them just excuses you're in the habit of using to keep from making a change, and not real roadblocks?

> **Constraints Insight Potential** - identifying what is truly blocking change and what is only self imposed or imagined limitations; enabling the problem-solver to make a choice for change based on the reality of their situation; informing the problem-solver as to the full set of requirements the solution must satisfy.

Once you clearly know what has prevented taking action before now, shift to thinking about what could be possible if the constraints were removed and the problem(s) solved. Discover what potential results would be exciting enough to cause you to want to find and implement a new solution.

Expectations/Excitement/Eagerness (E³) Questions – these questions are asked to learn what you expect or hope to experience as benefits by solving the problem and effectively implementing a new solution. The **E³** questions try to uncover your minimal expectations plus those benefits you really hope to achieve, and how eager you are to experience such benefits. The **E³** questions clarify your goal or goals and the deadline by which you want the problem(s) solved.

- What results do you think would meet your minimum expectations if you come up with a new solution?

- What is the most important thing you hope to gain with a new solution?

- What do you think would be the most exciting benefit of getting a solution that would fully meet your needs?

- If you are able to identify and implement the ideal solution, what would be the first thing you would like to brag about to your buddies?

- When do you hope to have the new solution in place?

- When must this problem be solved?

Expectation/Excitements/Eagerness (E³) Insight Potential – developing clarity about what the problem-solver really wants to achieve; elevating the problem-solver's expectations as to what could be achieved; bringing about a new energy and desire for better benefits; shifting motivation to an eagerness to discover how the improvement can be achieved; clarifying the deadline for when the problem must be solved; shifting from hesitation and resistance to a desire for action; and discovering new opportunities and possible results.

---

* * *

For each element of the $S.P.I.C.E^3$, I've presented many questions but I don't expect you to ask and answer all of them. Select a few for each element and answer each question to flesh out your problem definition. Spend half your time focused on fully understanding your own $S.P.I.C.E^3$.

This should take you through your own Reality Trough and the accompanying emotions as you address your problems, the costs of those problems, and what is keeping you stuck. As you explore the Reality Trough, notice and really feel the emotions associated with the realization that this problem is serious and deserves to be solved. Feel the low point of your situation. These feelings become the motivation to find a better solution and to achieve better results.

As you then explore the E^3 portion of your $S.P.I.C.E^3$, you will ascend to a more hopeful and excited place as you realize there are opportunities for benefits you hadn't considered before. If you do this, you should experience your motivation rising to find the best possible solution. In this place, you're ready for change. You will have a more complete understanding of where you are now, and where you would rather be. Your goals and deadline will be clear.

Techniques For Exploring The S.P.I.C.E³

There are different techniques that you can use to extract the information that is your S.P.I.C.E³ in order to arrive at a clear definition of the problem. You can do this alone, work with the significant others you've identified in Step Two, or seek another person who is not part of the problem to help you draw this information out.

S.P.I.C.E³ INTERVIEW

Pick a neutral third party who will act as an interviewer to draw the information out of the participants that share the problem. This will require a high level of trust on your part and some skill on the part of the person you select. He or she should have good listening skills and have a proficiency for making people feel comfortable when they talk about themselves.

Show this person the material in this book on the S.P.I.C.E³ elements and the questions that can be used to get the problem-solver talking about the problem. Ask this person to extract information from you by asking a few of these questions and then using active listening skills (invitations, paraphrases, inference checks, feelings checks, identification, and explained questions – see Appendix 2) to help you think out the problem definition and to express the information that makes up this problem.

Pick another person to act as a recorder of what you tell your interviewer or use some sort of recording device to capture what emerges. If more than one person is involved, it would be best if this information could be written on a large white board or flip chart sheets hung on a wall so everyone can see what has been said.

In response to this person's questions and active listening, express what you know about each of the five elements. Try to reach for information that is below your conscious awareness. Pay attention to any feelings that emerge as you hear and answer the questions. Get the information out and feel your way through the Reality Trough of your situation. In particular, feel the consequences of your unsolved problem, truly examine the roadblocks that have held you back from doing something about this before now, and notice what potential new results would really excite you. Don't just get the information. Notice how all of this expanded awareness makes you feel.

FIVE LISTS

Set a time frame in which you will produce information about the problem definition. This time limit should approximate half of the time you have available to work on this problem. Work on defining the problem by making lists of the five S.P.I.C.E³ elements until the time limit has elapsed. Try not to quit early.

If more than one participant is involved, place large sheets of paper on the wall and title each sheet with one of the S.P.I.C.E³ elements:

- Situation
- Problems
- Implications
- Constraints
- Expectations, Excitements, Eagerness (Goals and Deadline)

Appoint someone to be a recorder and have the participants generate information as it comes to mind and write the information down on the appropriate sheet. The person expressing the idea should say which sheet the idea is to be written on. The writer must record the words exactly as stated.

No participant needs to be thinking about the appropriateness of the information, it's accuracy or if it is placed in the correct section. Just produce the information as quickly as you can. Fill up the sheets. Start new ones if there is a surplus of information. Also write down any feelings that emerge, particularly as you explore the Implications and Constraints. Get a real understanding of the Reality Trough of your situation.

If the problem-solver is an individual, use copies of the sample S.P.I.C.E³ sheet in Appendix 3 and fill in information for each element of the S.P.I.C.E³ without regard for its accuracy or whether or not it pertains to the problem. Just describe as much as you can about each of the five elements. Note how you feel as you consider the Implications and Consequences – get a good handle on the reality of your situation. Feel the low point of your Reality Trough.

Fill in the sheets as comprehensively as possible. Include all information during this first phase. Don't worry or slow yourself down trying to get the items listed in any logical order. As a piece of information emerges, just get it written down. Work to get to as solid a definition of the problem as you can achieve.

ZEN MAP

Take the image showing what a problem definition entails as shown on page 58 and place it on a large whiteboard, leaving room to record information around the image. Then sit still, and quietly meditate on your problem. As ideas emerge in your thoughts, write them on the sheet outside the oval and draw an arrow to where the information belongs in the problem definition. If more than one person is dong this, then each person would have a pen and write their own thoughts down as they surface.

The information that has to do with where you are now (Situation, Problems, Implications and Constraints) should all be placed on the left side of the oval, and the information that has to do with where you would like to be (the goal in the form of minimal expectations, the highly desirable benefits that would excite you, and when you would like to achieve these by) would all be on the right side of the oval. Fill this map out until you feel that you have been sitting quietly for a few minutes without any new ideas emerging.

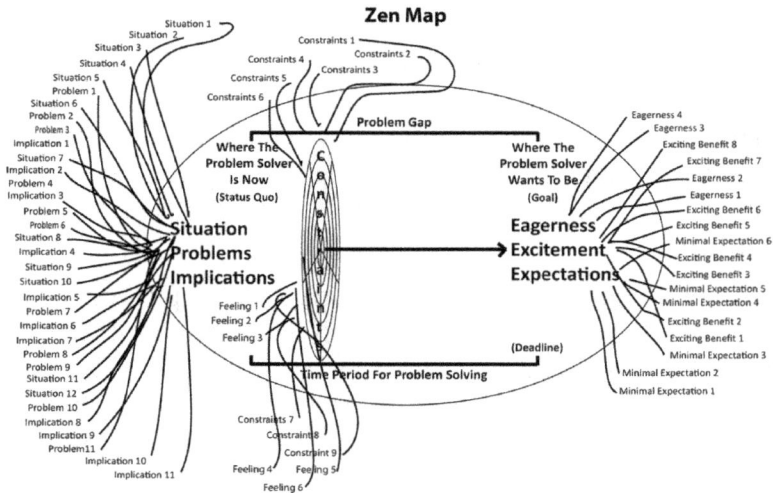

Zen Map

Then study the map to get a concentrated understanding of all that comprises the problem that you are going to try to solve. You should review it in the S.P.I.C.E^3 order and feel the Reality Trough – the low point of your current situation – and then flow through to the high point of excitement and eagerness.

3x5 CARDS

Get a deck of 3x5 cards and five small boxes. Label each of the boxes with one of the five elements:

- Situation
- Problem
- Implications
- Constraints
- Expectations/Excitements/Eagerness (Goals and Deadline)

On each card, write down one bit of information about your problem then throw the card into the appropriate box. If more than one person is doing this, each person would work on their own cards separately then throw them into the correct box. Do this for at least ten minutes. Do it longer if the problem is complex. Continue until the ten minutes is up, or if going longer, until five minutes have passed without any ideas going into a box.

Take the cards out of each respective box and post them on a cork board or wall in columns under the titles of the five elements. Take time to study each column. If any new ideas emerge, write them on a card and add them. If more than one person is involved, discuss the information, come to an agreement that it fits within the problem definition, and arrive at a shared understanding of the problem that you are going to solve together.

PROBLEM STATEMENT

If the problem-solver is an individual, just write out a problem solving statement in S.P.I.C.E^3 order. Be as succinct as you can about each element but try to be inclusive of information. Make sure to include underutilized resources in the statement of your situation, and focus on the feelings you have as you specify the problems, implications and constraints. Be very specific about what you would like to achieve by solving this problem.

If the problem-solver is a couple or group, discuss the S.P.I.C.E[3] then work together to arrive at a clear statement that defines the problem you are going to work on. Because this approach isn't very structured, there is a greater potential for conflict as you do this, so the participants need to adopt an attitude of cooperation as opposed to one of resistance for this to flow smoothly.

HERE NOW – WANT TO BE THERE

If you are having trouble defining the problem in terms of the S.P.I.C.E[3], then do this simpler version to arrive at something similar. Set a time limit. On a large piece of paper, draw three columns:

Here Now	Can't Because	Want To Be There

Then fill in the three columns with as much information as you can. First describe what "Here Now" looks like. Then describe what "There" would look like. Once you have filled in those two columns, then list all the reasons that you aren't already "There". Don't worry about having any logical order to the points. Just list as much information as possible in the time you set. Once the time has elapsed, then look at the three lists, and do a fourth:

What Does It Cost If This Problem Goes Unsolved

List whatever you think it currently costs in the situation you are in right now and whatever benefits you might be missing. If you do this, you will be close to a S.P.I.C.E[3] definition of your problem. One significant missing piece is to declare the deadline by which you would really like to be "There". Set a deadline.

When To Move To The Next Step

In this model, the problem-solver needs to be able to briefly describe the situation, the problem and cause of symptoms, the true costs of the problem, and the constraints or roadblocks that keep the problem-solver stuck in his or her current situation. As well, the problem-solver needs to arrive at a list of minimum expectations and the exciting outcomes or benefits that the problem-solver would like to achieve by solving the problem. The excitement and eagerness to solve this problem must be present.

You're ready to move to the next step when you have a clear synopsis of the full problem definition. Once the problem-solver, or all problem-solving participants, fully know, understand, and agree on the S.P.I.C.E^3, it's time to initiate creative thinking about solution possibilities. When the problem-solver fully understands his or her S.P.I.C.E^3, move to the next step.

Transition To The Next Step

If the problem-solver is a group, you need to check that everyone understands and agrees on the S.P.I.C.E^3 by saying something like:

"I believe that we've fully defined the problem, and now know enough about the S.P.I.C.E^3 to begin the process of generating solution possibilities. Is everyone else in agreement that we can now look for solution possibilities that would produce (*the E^3 results*)."

If you are problem-solving on your own, then ask yourself:

"Do I clearly understand the gap between where I am now and what I want to achieve, the implications of staying the same, the constraints that I actually have to overcome, and what would be really exciting if I could achieve it?"

In either case, if the answer is "No", then you need to back up and fill in more of the missing information that describes the situation, problem(s), implications, constraints, and highly desirable benefits. In addition, there needs to be a clear indication as to when the problem should be solved.

Again, in either case, if the answer is "Yes", then move to the next step and determine which technique will be used to generate solution ideas.

"Great, so we need to figure out how we want to do the next step."

or

"Okay. It's now time to generate some solution ideas."

Step Four:
Generate Solution Possibilities

As a problem-solver, you are richer when there is more than one alternative to consider. In fact, the chance of finding an optimum solution rises extensively with the consideration of many possibilities. This process of generating more than one useful alternative can be fun and creative. There are many alternative techniques that can be used to generate many solution ideas. Done right, this step will yield a surplus of ideas.

Insight Potential When "Generating Solution Possibilities" – When this step is done right, you are more likely to discover a solution that is both innovative and superior to other ideas. When done effectively, you move beyond consideration of run-of-the-mill possibilities to creative thinking where the unexpected has a chance to emerge. You have an opportunity to achieve a real breakthrough, to find a solution that hadn't been considered before by anyone else but is obviously the best solution once it has been discovered. You have the opportunity to invent a new way of doing what you do.

Up until now, you've predominantly been using your conscious thinking to sort out what you know about the problem. However, if you used the presented techniques, your subconscious mind also had opportunities to bring up information, poking it into conscious awareness and uncovering some of the hidden information. You gathered information as you examined the five key elements.

In this mindset, you sorted through facts looking for new insights about your S.P.I.C.E[3]. Desirably, you also did this in such a way that allowed feelings to emerge – the feelings of frustration and discomfort when you recognized the real costs of the way things are now, and the feelings of excitement when you identified the potentially new benefits you might achieve if you could find the ideal solution to your problem.

Now it's time to stimulate your creative juices to consider a very broad range of possibilities. Suspend your focus on facts, put to sleep your critical thinking, and open up your mind. The thinking of our conscious mind generally revolves around normal everyday thoughts. These thoughts are targeted at sustaining the status quo and not imagining a new and better world.

The conscious mind tends to come up with typical ideas, and immediately judges them as either appropriate or not. The goal of the conscious mind is to find an acceptable solution and move on. If an idea isn't immediately judged to be a good one, the idea is discarded.

One fallacy too many people hold to be true is that they just need to identify one adequate solution and move on. This can be like the driver that turns out of a traffic jam onto a road that doesn't really lead to their destination just to keep moving. Coming up with only one 'somewhat-acceptable' alternative in order to have the illusion that the problem is being dealt with, turns out to be self-defeating.

The subconscious mind however, can entertain the impossible, the fantastical, the unusual. Our subconscious is the dwelling of fantasy, dreams, imagination. We want to tap into that type of thinking. If we expand the boundaries to include more ideas, we have a greater probability that the best solution(s) will emerge.

Solution generation is a distinct step in the problem-solving process and no other activities should be allowed to encroach on the process of just generating new ideas. During this step, you are no longer questioning whether or not a problem exists, defining the problem, or wondering what it is that you are trying to achieve. Similarly, you are not determining which is the best idea, making a decision, or prepping to implement any one idea. In this step, you are just generating a list of possible (and even impossible) solution ideas.

For effective problem-solving to occur, our critical thinking must be temporarily suspended to free up our imagination and open the door for creative ideas to emerge in the same way that we normally produce fantasies and dreams. By setting aside a requirement that ideas must be logical or must immediately meet a standard of good quality, the mind is allowed to form creative associations.

These associations might actually be weak as solution ideas on their own, but when liberated, act as a bridge to ideas that might not have readily been considered. These unusual ideas may subsequently turn out to be the most effective resolutions to the problem.

By setting aside logic and our normal critical thinking processes, we are better able to realize insight and arrive at a solution that would not normally have been considered, one that turns out to obviously be the best solution once identified. Such 'ah ah' ideas come from a different order of thinking compared to what has kept the problem-solver mired in the problem up to this point.

In this step you will now think about as many solution possibilities as you can, particularly including those solutions that might appear to border on the impossible. By setting aside the need for an idea to be a good idea, your mind opens up and many more ideas can emerge. More ideas means more latitude to generate a solution that is very different from anything considered before.

Goals For The Solution Generation Step

This step involves only one activity – generating ideas that could be possible solutions to the problem. The goals at this step in the problem-solving process are to:

- produce a list of as many ideas as possible,

- at least 30% of those ideas, at first glance, should be very unusual, weird, imaginative, possibly impossible, maybe not even related to the defined problem,

- have fun getting creative, and

- generate ideas that ultimately arrive at no fewer than three optimum solution possibilities.

At this step, we aren't looking for just one solution but several that are of high quality, each capable of achieving the desired E^3 outcomes. We don't limit ourselves by only pursuing one solution – expand your own opportunities by reaching for several.

Techniques For Solution Generation

There are various techniques that a problem-solver can use to develop a large list of ideas. These approaches clearly require that all evaluation of ideas is suspended, and the focus is exclusively upon generating as many ideas as possible.

BRAINSTORMING

In order to achieve the best possible solution, one that achieves the full E^3 outcomes, many novel and creative ideas must be generated. The principle process for this creative thinking is called brainstorming. Brainstorming is a term initially popularized by Alex F. Osborn in the book *Applied Imagination*, based on his work with groups working on advertising campaigns. This is now the most commonly used technique for solution generation. Overtime, specific rules of conduct have emerged:

1. Set a definite time period for solution generation and generate ideas throughout (Stick to that time limit).

2. Use a time period for solution generation that parallels the significance and difficulty of the problem.

3. Think of and say out loud as many ideas as you can in the time allowed.

4. Think of unusual, far out, imaginative, even absurd ideas.

5. Suspend all censorship – there should be no evaluation or criticism of any idea during this period.

6. Record all ideas as they are said out loud, without censorship or modification in the act of recording each idea.

7. Record even those ideas that the recorder might think have been expressed already.

and

8. Cheer yourself on and make encouraging comments about the growing number of ideas – not the quality of the ideas themselves.

Each of these rules has a very deliberate purpose. The objective is to free up your creative thinking, thereby increasing your potential to arrive at an optimum solution. These rules have been shaped by various underlying principles.

1. Many Ideas

Consider how difficult the problem appears to be, how costly the status quo really is, how stuck the problem-solvers feel, and set a target for a large enough number of ideas that true creative thinking can achieve. For a minor problem, perhaps only thirty ideas must be generated. For a moderate problem, the objective might be set as at least fifty ideas.

For solving very costly problems where great benefits could be realized by discovering an optimal solution, the objective should be higher. Where the problem is very important, task yourself to generate at least one hundred ideas, retaining the goal of having at least thirty percent of these ideas striking you as creative, unusual, possibly absurd.

2. Fantastical Thinking

Free up your mind to quickly generate thoughts. Give yourself permission to say out loud whatever comes to mind, trusting your subconscious to make associations that your conscious mind would never consider.

Initial ideas will likely be solutions you've seen in action before. You want to move beyond such ideas because they have likely already been rejected as suitable solutions, or they would have already been implemented and the necessary changes made. Just as you shouldn't hold back the fantastical ideas, don't hold back the normal, common-sense ideas because the sooner such ideas have been stated, the sooner you will be able to move forward to new, atypical, creative ideas. This process of generating fantastical ideas moves in waves.

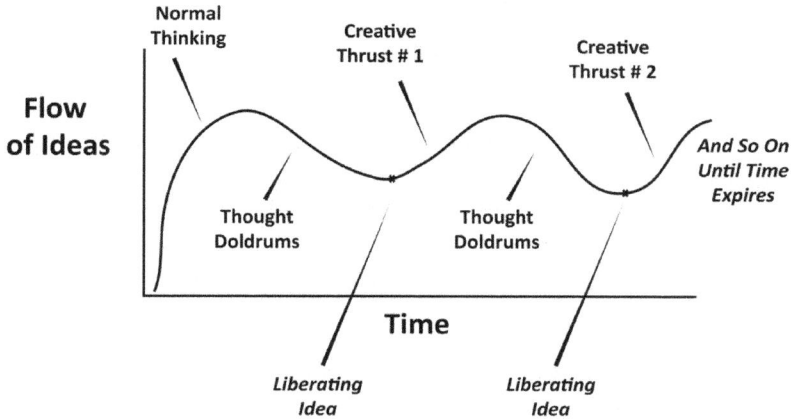

Initially, there is likely to be a rush of ideas as the process starts, although for some people, couples and groups, there can be a delay until they can shift mental gears and adopt the rule of just thinking of ideas without evaluation. Too often, people start out thinking they have to come up with a good idea and spin their wheels trying to think what that could be. However, once they loosen up and just say what comes to mind, there will be an initial rush of ideas, possibly coming so quickly that it is difficult to record them. These ideas are seldom far-out creative ideas, but may be.

More typically, this first rush of ideas produces possibilities that are relatively typical, normal, less than fantastical ideas. They come, and then the rush of ideas slows down as the first of the "Thought Doldrums" sets in. This moment of growing quiet can leave the problem-solver thinking that he or she has run out of ideas. Because these "Thought Doldrums" occur, the other rules of brainstorming keep the process going.

The problem-solver is charged with saying whatever comes to mind, and to try to think of unusual associations to the problem. Our minds wander and it is this wandering that takes place in the doldrums and allows new material to emerge into consciousness. The association with the problem may not be obvious or even exist at this time but if the problem-solver states out loud what has come to mind, this causes other associations to form.

For example, a problem-solver in a group setting may experience his thinking about the problem slow down and begin to think about the Peanut Butter and Jam sandwich he has planned for lunch. By saying peanut butter out loud, others in the group might be taken to other associations as they wonder why he said peanut butter – unconsciously consider its substance (density, color, texture, taste, smell, liquidity); or consider its origin (mashed nuts, sugar, puréed, jarred, taken from the ground, husks, bunches): or recall a childhood memory (Mom, school, trading or sharing with others, allergic reactions, hunger, toast); or make any other associations because the list of possibilities is unlimited.

Such associations lead to new thoughts and ideas that must also be stated out loud. These further stimulate the thinking of others and take the idea flow out of the doldrums into a new creative thrust of ideas. Such unusual or "out of apparent context" ideas liberate other ideas to emerge and a new creative thrust takes place. The doldrums come, and then there are new wave crests as free associations stimulate new creative ideas.

3. No Evaluation

If an idea is immediately put to the test, then the process bogs down with questions like:

- Is the idea logical?
- Is the idea good enough?
- Will this work?
- Will everybody support the idea?

Only a few ideas have an opportunity to surface in such a challenging environment. These ideas are seldom revolutionary and lead to less than satisfactory outcomes. Instead of bringing about a higher order change, these supposed solution ideas tend to be more of the same and the problem is only marginally modified – not truly solved.

This key rule forces us into different thinking. Instead of critical analysis as each idea surfaces, we simply allow each idea to trigger new ideas. If instead, by following the rule of no evaluation, we create a welcoming climate, where ideas of any quality are encouraged, allowed to step into consciousness, reach the recorded list, and serve to stimulate other ideas, more ideas emerge and the chances of finding an optimum solution increase.

4. Record All Ideas

Get the ideas out of your mind by saying them aloud and record them exactly as they are expressed, then move on to the next idea. By recording each idea, the problem-solver doesn't have to worry about remembering the idea, doesn't have to think about its value, and doesn't have to stop generating new ideas because that idea can be reviewed once the solution generation step is completed.

By recording every idea, all ideas are treated as equal at this stage, giving each idea an opportunity to be fully considered later in the problem-solving process. If the problem-solver is a group, this means that every member will be heard, and their ideas respected. This creates a cooperative atmosphere, which contrasts sharply with the competitive atmosphere of most group situations. If the problem-solver is a couple, this rule is a leveler, giving equal power to both partners. If the problem-solver is an individual, this rule allows an opportunity for all of the different and sometimes conflicted desires and the different voices in one's head to generate creative possibilities that could lead to a solution.

By recording all ideas, we create a list of ideas to be considered more fully in the next step in the problem-solving process. Instead of considering only one or two or three ideas, the problem-solver is setting the stage for an analytical assessment of widely different options. This significantly increases the chances that the best solution, the solution that satisfies both minimal expectations and the most desired benefits, will be discovered.

5. Even Record Apparent Duplicates

In some cases, an idea might emerge which seems to just be a duplicate of something previously recorded. Record it anyway and in the exact words in which it is expressed. Excluding this idea is a form of censorship killing further idea generation.

In addition, the decision to exclude would mean a rejection by the recorder who thinks the ideas are the same when there may be a kernel of difference that could be important. Each idea should be treated as different because it could quite possibly be. On the other hand, the idea might be the same as one previously stated and by recording it twice, there is a possibility that later in the evaluation step this idea will be given deeper consideration because the subconscious mind of the problem-solver thought enough of the idea to have it emerge twice.

6. Encourage Quantity – Not Quality

By focusing on the goal of generating many ideas, we again add to this climate of cooperation, this climate of creative and lateral thinking. This furthers the chances that an optimum solution will be freed from the problem-solver's subconscious. By praising the flow of ideas, the problem-solver feels rewarded for creative and lateral thinking, and hears permission to come up with more of what the critical mind might consider to be weird, too far-out, and even absurd or impossible ideas.

Such idea generation is crucial to success so encouraging quantity out loud further enhances the atmosphere of unfettered idea generation. Cheer yourself on to more ideas. Demand 10 more, 20 more and so on. Continuously stress the need for more ideas while there is still time to generate them.

7. Set A Time Period and Stick To It

Because thought doldrums occur, it can seem to the problem-solver that there are no more useful ideas. This is a fallacy. There are always more ideas if one follows the other rules, forms other associations as the mind wanders in the quiet periods and states out loud what emerges. Sticking to a time limit means the problem-solver will not quit this step prematurely.

The time period can be extended if more ideas keep emerging and the overall deadline for solving the problem allows an extension. However, the time should not be cut short. The doldrums allow re-generation of creative juices and it is typical that the mind needs moments of quiet and distraction to rejuvenate a new line of thinking. Instead of stopping when it seems like the flow of ideas has run down, wait. Eventually new ideas emerge and liberate others.

8. Time Period Should Match The Significance Of The Problem

Begin this step with a clear declaration of how much time will be dedicated to generation of solution possibilities. The difficulty and significance of the problem will determine how much time you will need. Set a longer time for this step when the problem is very important and/or believed to be a very tough problem to solve.

Recommended Time For Brainstorming

The Problem Is...	The Problem Is Perceived	
	As Possible Of Solution	As Impossible Until Now
Very Important	15-30 Minutes *more than 50 ideas*	Over A Minimum of Three Days *more than 100 ideas*
Low In Importance	5-10 Minutes *more than 10 ideas*	10-20 Minutes *more than 30 ideas*

If the problem is very basic and perceived to not have much difficulty at all, set a time period of five or ten minutes. On the other hand, if the existing problem is very costly and believed to be difficult to solve, set a long enough time frame that there are rest and sleep intervals between the brainstorming sessions, and even time for other completely distracting events like other work, games of sport, totally unrelated conversations, listening to music, watching something dramatic like a play or movie, reading passages in unrelated reading material.

A very challenging problem might require a brainstorming period of three days if the deadline will allow. You need a longer time frame to allow the subconscious processes to generate ideas that just won't come from the conscious mind. This subconscious contribution comes during naps, periods of just drifting off, distracting ourselves completely from the problem through play, or overnight as we sleep.

9. Side Benefit of Brainstorming By Multiple Problem-Solvers

When a group of people engage in the non-evaluative generation of ideas, there is less likelihood that individuals will get locked into their own ideas. The group generally feels pride in having come up with so many alternatives, some of which surprised them but stand out as quality possibilities. Instead of thinking their way is the best way, the participants are now more open to finding the truly best solution.

In typical problem-solving situations, one person expresses an idea, others critique it and the idea presenter has to defend his or her idea. This tends to lock the idea presenter into supporting that idea and only that idea. Someone else does the same and we have two opposing ideas, with the resulting disagreement. A third or fourth compromise idea might emerge until the argument is supposedly resolved as the group picks the safest alternative. However, commitment to the idea by all parties is usually weak at best.

Brainstorming in the solution generation step, with the total suspension of evaluation and the concomitant arguing, leads to a highly cooperative climate in the group. Members' minds are opened up to many ideas and they will then want to determine which of the many are the best solution for their problem.

STIMULUS TRICKS

There are things that can be done to shake up the problem-solver's thinking when it seems like a doldrum period is going on too long. Look for something unrelated to the problem that can be used as a stimulus for free association. For example, it can be any object on your table or in the room:

- A book – how does the topic relate to potential solutions?

- Stationary or a stationary tool such as a stapler – how does what the stapler looks like, does, feels like, or accomplish, relate to potential solutions?

- A chair or the table itself – what about the chair or table design might apply, about the purpose of the chair or table, the components of a chair or table?

- A Picture or the Picture Frame – any associations come to mind?

- A Word in A Dictionary – how could the meaning of this word lead to solution ideas and new associations?

Free associate. Just say what ever comes to mind. If you are using a cup, think about what the cup does that might somehow relate to a solution for your problem.

Alternatively, change your problem-solving environment. If you are inside, go out. If in one room, move to another. If you're working in the morning, stop and continue later in the day, perhaps at a place to eat or play.

There are many other sources of association stimuli. You could just throw out the name of a TV show, or a movie. You could look out the window and see a vehicle pass by and use the name of the vehicle. Look up, down, behind you, sideways and name what you see or hear. Think of a bodily function and name it (eat, breath, cough, smell, fart, jump, etc).

If you've set a longer period for this step, you can look to others for input. Find your stimulus for free association by talking to others that have nothing to do with the problem and invite them to free associate as you describe the S.P.I.C.E[3] of this problem. Turn to children and explain your problem as simply as you can, then invite their thoughts. Children love to think creatively, and have less internal censorship. You're not asking them to solve the problem – just seeking their thoughts about what could be done to solve it, and hoping what they offer is quite random. After you've collected thoughts from others, sit down on your own and think about how their thoughts lead you to new ideas.

Use the creative output of others to stimulate your own thinking. Turn to music, a book of fiction, a movie or theatrical play. Stop and just devote your attention to the music, book, movie or play without expecting yourself to come up with ideas. Once finished, take some free time, again without having to think about any solution ideas. Let the creative material you've just encountered percolate in your subconscious mind, which will find associations to the problem over the resting period. Then return to your brainstorming and see what new ideas emerge.

REVERSE THINKING

If you notice that many solution ideas appear to be heading in one direction, then set a goal of coming up with at least ten reverse ideas, or ideas that go in a different direction. For example, working on the goal of improving health care services, a group might be brainstorming many ideas that center around building a new hospital. It might be time to say, "Stop – let's look for at least ten ideas in a different direction." This might produce a flow of ideas like:

- A Hospital On Wheels – complete with roving doctor and nurse, hospital bed and accessories to be left in the patient's home, various mobile diagnostic tools and equipment, a portable pharmacy, and more.

- A Hospital In A Box – to be delivered to the patients home by a master triage nurse to allow first stage diagnostics and treatment.

- Create a fund that rewards people for healthy practices and "low-to-no need" for hospital services during their lifetimes.

- Medicentres in every ten city block radius where all medical services except intensive care surgery can be provided including full diagnostics.

- More auxiliary care homes with 24hr nursing services to allow relocation from existing hospitals of patients who are chronically ill but not requiring emergency services, thereby clearing space in existing hospitals.

- Several emergency-only clinics with full diagnostic services and bed service for a maximum of three days before removal to an auxiliary facility.

- Open opium dens instead and place those who are chronically ill, or the elderly who are suffering from severe illness, and provide only comfort care or end of life care.

- A contract with a hotel chain to operate bed services in facilities adjacent to medicentres.

- Ambulance services complete with doctors, nurses and Emergency Medical Technicians.

- Refuse admission to hospital with anything less than a life threatening illness, to be determined at a Triage entrance.

- Provide an auxiliary income to those that never need to use medical services for the treatment of illness.

- Build studies in naturopathic treatment into all high school programs.

- And so on.

The objective isn't to criticize the previous ideas but to change the focus, to bring about a new stream of creativity. Calling out, "Reverse Thinking" should only be done if many ideas have already been produced and a participant thinks that the group is stuck in a singular focus on what could potentially solve the problem.

THE NOMINAL GROUP TECHNIQUE (NGT)

Originally developed by Andre Delbecq and Andrew H. Van de Ven, the nominal group technique can be used to generate many ideas when problem-solving in group situations. The Nominal Group Technique was developed for use in community development work where groups could involve hundreds of people. It can be used where any group is five people or more. If there are many people, break them into five person groups and have each group work separately.

By its nature, NGT is slower and conducted in a calmer atmosphere than all out brainstorming, and this can be helpful to those people that need more time to think of their own ideas. There are two phases of the NGT Technique that fall into the Solution Generation Step. The third takes place later during Evaluation. However, of importance now, there are two specific steps to follow for an NGT brainstorm.

Step One: Individual Work

Have each member write a list of their own solution possibilities on their own fresh sheet of paper during a five or ten minute time period. Encourage each person to privately follow the brainstorming rule of no evaluation, and to come up with as many far-out ideas as they can.

Step Two: Group Work

Gather all individuals into groups of five or six people. Tell the participants that this phase if for the purpose of building a longer list of ideas.

- use a recording medium such as blackboard, whiteboard, flip chart, or computer with screen image projected on the wall,

- have each member take a turn and share one idea from their list,

- record the idea exactly as it was expressed,

- interrupt any attempt to discuss an idea, and emphasize the importance of just collecting ideas,

- continue in round-robin order having each member either express an idea, or when it is their turn, indicate that they wish to pass for this round, and

- continue in round-robin fashion until all members say pass.

By using this slower, more deliberate process, each member has an opportunity to contribute. This will take more time so double the time period set for brainstorming.

GET IDEAS FROM EXPERTS

One option for any problem-solver is to turn to experts who have knowledge and experience in dealing with problems similar in nature to the problem-solver's current problem. If the problem-solver thinks he or she just doesn't have the expertise to deal with the problem, then there can be value in turning to others, those who have prior experience and confidence in their knowledge.

The expert could be a boss, someone who has experienced the problem before on a personal level, a student who studies in the problem area, or a professional consultant. You will likely need to explain that you wish to use him or her as a supportive resource and that you aren't just handing the problem over. Emphasize that you retain responsibility for solving the problem.

To retain ownership of the problem and to feel fully responsible for getting the problem solved, we recommend the following approach:

- on your own, complete both "step one – felt need", "step two – include relevant others", and "step three – define the problem" before looking for outside assistance,

- turn to more than one expert (try to include three or more),

- present the full description of the S.P.I.C.E[3] for this problem to each expert,

- ask each expert to generate five possible solutions to the problem as you have presented it, to fully list each idea with a complete clarification and elaboration so the idea is fully fleshed out,

- ask each expert to develop at least one fantastical and innovative possibility that might cause you to go "ah-ha",

- tell the expert you are not asking him or her to recommend the solution he or she thinks is best, but to just come up with five possibilities that he or she likes,

- give these experts a very specific deadline by which they must get you their list of ideas,

- generate your own list of five possible solutions with full clarification and elaboration, with a focus on trying to think of ridiculous and outlandish ideas,

- collect the list of at least five possible solutions from each expert and mix their ideas with your own, and

- move to the next step which involves equally evaluating all ideas (your own count as much as those produced by experts because you are the real expert in your own situation).

This approach is quite different from what might typically occur when expert consultants are contracted to solve problems. Usually, we turn over all of the problem-solving process to the expert and wait passively for them to tell us what to do. They both define the problem and come up with their own selection of what the expert believes is the best solution.

The weakness of that typical approach is that the person or persons who have the actual problem, and those who will implement the solution, are not as committed to the solution as the expert. With less commitment, there is a real risk that the solution will be less effectively implemented and fail to produce the desired outcomes that the problem-solver might have achieved if he or she solved the problem on his or her own.

By working in this way, the real problem-solver retains ownership and control over his or her own problem and is responsible for deciding what to do and how to fully implement the solution. This increases the problem-solver's expertise both through the input obtained from experts and from completing the problem-solving process on his or her own.

When To Move To The Next Step

You will know it's time to move on when the specified period of time for brainstorming has elapsed or when the idea flow has stopped, which ever is later. In general, you want to achieve at least the following number of ideas for each problem type before you move on:

Problem is not important and seen as easy to solve	10+
Problem is not that important but seen as very tough	30+
Problem is very important but seen as solvable	50+
Problem is very important but seen as almost impossible	100

Do not move on before time has expired and do not move on if ideas are still coming at a satisfying pace. More ideas help, not hurt. In fact, even if you move on and the problem-solver subsequently has a new idea, add it to the list.

Depending on how you recorded the ideas during this step, you may need to do a bit of touch up work to arrive at a workable list that all participants can readily see. Take the list and work on it so that the ideas are clear and bold on the page. Do not edit them or change them in any way. Put the ideas on a large sheet of paper (or many if many ideas) and post the sheet(s) on the wall so they are easy to see and read. Alternatively, the ideas can be entered into a spreadsheet or word processor in a large font and displayed on a wall for all to see.

Transition To The Next Step

You have a list of ideas but you don't yet have full understanding of the ideas, and the ideas are not as fleshed out as they need to be. In the next step, the problem-solver will work on each idea to make sure that all elements are clear and the idea has been expanded to what it could fully entail.

Indicate that it's time to shift focus to clarify and elaborate each of the ideas. For an individual, this amounts to recognizing that it is time to clarify, elaborate and expand each idea without being critical of the idea in any way. For a group of problem-solvers, this could involve one of the participants saying something like:

"We've got a lot of possibilities written down but they're just idea kernels right now. We need to look at each one, clarify it, elaborate on it, expand each idea into a workable solution."

Step Five:
Elaborate

There is a normal tendency to immediately criticize and evaluate ideas, putting them up against measuring sticks such as "Is it logical?, "Is it too expensive?", "Will it work?", "Will others accept it?", or even "Do you like it?" These are important considerations that a solution must satisfy before being selected as the solution to be put into practice, but when these questions are asked too soon, and when ideas are still immature and not fully formed, too many ideas get rejected too soon. Problem-solving is enhanced when kernels of ideas are clarified, expanded, elaborated on, even added to other ideas so that they are given fair consideration before being critically evaluated.

Insight Potential When "Elaborating" – *Weak ideas when clarified, expanded upon, elaborated, added to other ideas to make a better whole, have the chance to emerge and potentially become the optimal solution. An idea that at first glance might be rejected has the opportunity upon deeper consideration to become the innovative solution that yields exceptional results. Expanding ideas, fleshing them out, and pulling ideas together increases the chances of discovering optimum solutions.*

By now, you should have a large list of ideas – more if the problem is perceived as difficult. Most of these ideas emerged as brief thoughts and were written down as such. Many may not be all that clear so it is important to get clarity before evaluating the idea to assess its appropriateness as a solution. Once the idea has been clarified, expanded, and fully understood by the problem-solver, then and only then, can it be critiqued.

Once again, we are delaying all criticism and any attempt to select the final solution. We want the optimum solution, and at this point we only have a list of possibilities – many of which are not yet completely understood and many of which are not fully expanded ideas. Premature evaluation would kill most of these ideas.

Unfortunately, this step is very atypical when you listen to most people try to solve their problems. Most people come up with just a few ideas and pick the most acceptable (least controversial) of the few. This step is often skipped as people race on to pick one of the ideas that emerged. As a result, the solution is typically not thought out as well as it should be and there is a real danger that the optimum solution will have been missed and something lesser put into action. But if the problem-solver could consider many ideas and ultimately pick the most optimum solution, results should be significantly better.

Goals Of The Elaboration Step

As a problem-solver that wants to maximize the likelihood that an optimum solution will be found, you have several goals at this step:

- Elaborate and expand on <u>all</u> ideas so they are seen in their best light and all potential elements of the idea are brought into awareness.

- Clarify <u>all</u> ideas as if they all have tremendous implications for the optimum solution of our problem.

- Prevent any premature evaluation of ideas that fall into the category of appearing to be too far-out, impossible, weird.

- Inhibit rejection of ideas as unworkable before they are fully understood and expanded.

and

- Flesh out creative ideas to the degree that they become optimum solution possibilities.

This step is within the first half of our problem-solving sequence because we are still looking for creative thinking. The brainstorming mentality should continue as the ideas are clarified, expanded, elaborated and merged to make viable solutions.

In some cases, the brainstorm in the Generation of Solutions Step was so successful, the problem-solver hits this Elaboration step and thinks it would be way too much work to clarify and elaborate on every idea. If the problem is seen as one of lower significance, if the problem is seen as quite possible to solve, or if the deadline is so dire that problem-solving must move rapidly, then the goals would include:

- Arrive at a short list of enough fleshed out ideas with seventy percent comprised of those seen as potentially workable solutions (70%), and about thirty percent of ideas that at first appeared to be a real stretch (30%).

The primary objective is to retain and flesh out as many of the ideas generated in the solution generation step so that chances of finding optimum solution opportunities are as high as possible. Rejection of ideas before they are fully understood and expanded leads to loss of useful information; and, if the problem-solver is a couple or group, can lead to conflict over which ideas to retain instead of cooperation to find the best solution(s).

Strategies For Reducing The Number Of Ideas At This Stage

At this stage it is easy to feel overwhelmed with the number of ideas. The ideal process would be to clarify and expand every idea. However, if the problem-solver feels that there are too many ideas and this would take too long, then there are various strategies to reduce the list to a manageable number, while saving the most creative ideas for consideration.

The problem-solver is advised to deliberately preserve and clarify at least some of the creative ideas. Ideas that at first glance appear to be too far-out, absurd, impossible, ridiculous, or weird, may in fact be the kernel of the most optimum solution. So the weeding out criteria should be based on something like "either there is too little there to see a potential solution in what has been written down, or the recorded item is obviously just a stimulus idea that was expressed during a Thought Doldrum to spark the flow of new ideas."

If the problem is thought to be relatively easy, or if a solution has to be found relatively quickly, then keep and consider at least twenty (20) ideas. If the problem is considered to be almost impossible, or there is a large amount of time to find the optimum solution, then clarify and expand at least fifty (50) ideas. Preserve the original lists because it may prove necessary to return and revisit more if the reduced list doesn't result in an optimum solution as you proceed.

There are various ways to reduce the list or organize it so it is a more manageable list to take forward to clarification and elaboration.

- Look for and cross off the trigger ideas that are obviously just trigger ideas (for example, if *peanut butter* appears on your list, cross it off).

- Set a minimum number of ideas to be taken further and group together any ideas that have similar elements – work down to groups of similar ideas.

- Cross off those ideas that have been tried before, are expressed only as idea fragments, or ideas that have no support by the problem-solver for further consideration.

- If the problem-solver is a couple or group, allow each member to privately take time to chose ten ideas they would want considered further. Then once each person has identified their own ten, have him or her place check marks by each of the selected ideas on the public list. All members would do this at the same time so the members aren't influencing each other. Build a new list by writing down the ideas that have check marks beside them. This will likely result in a list shorter than (number of members X 10) because some ideas will have been checked multiple times.

- Pick a set number of what appear to be possible solution ideas and then pick the same set number of what seems to be fantastical. For example, you might select ten (10) ideas that seem practicable. Then pick the same number of ideas (10) that seem to be far-out, absurd, weird, never considered before, ideas. Now take these ideas (20 in the example) and elaborate and clarify them.

- If the problem-solver is a couple or group, give each member a moment to pick a set number of ideas that they would like to reject at this time. For example, if the list is huge, give each person the chance to identify 20 rejects. Then, each person would share one of his or her rejections in round-robin fashion. If any one vetoes the rejection, the idea stays. There is no need to explain the veto. Just say, "I veto that rejection." If no one vetoes the rejection, the idea would be discarded. It is recommended that the idea be copied onto a 3x5 card and saved separately, but crossed off the master list. This round-robin process continues until each person has shared his or her rejection list.

Be aware though that the problem-solver runs the risk of throwing out optimum solutions because of a premature censorship. Instead, if possible, work forward with as many ideas as you can manage. So, only if the problem-solver needs a shorter list to work with, use one of the techniques to get that shorter list, then proceed with this step.

Now Elaborate And Clarify

At this point you have a list of ideas to be considered further. You do not have a list of solutions yet, and should not have narrowed your selection to just a few ideas. Ideally, you have both creative and practical ideas to expand and clarify with no allegiances to any particular idea or ideas. You want to proceed with an open mind. Set out in this stage to elaborate and expand ideas so that the optimum solution(s) can emerge.

The objective is to suspend censorship, criticism, and selection until all ideas have seen enough of the light of day to be given a fair evaluation. The ideas aren't yet clear. They are just thought kernels and need more elaboration. The goal is to make sure the problem-solver fully understands an idea and all of its potential elements to fairly evaluate the idea.

This is particularly important when the problem-solver is a couple or group. Everyone must share a common understanding of the idea before they cast a vote on its applicability as a solution. If the idea has not yet been clarified, there is too much room for conflicts to emerge over which idea is better and such a conflict would be based on misunderstanding rather than substantive disagreement.

The rules for this stage are:

1. Make no selection of a solution at this time.

2. Elaborate and expand on all ideas – do not cut the process short.

3. Merge ideas that are complimentary to each other.

4. Clarify all ideas, allowing all thoughts about what the idea means to surface.

5. No evaluation, censorship, or criticism of any idea.

Presumably, you have your recorded list of ideas. It is now time to create a new recording sheet, an Elaboration and Clarification chart, which looks like the following:

IDEA	ELABORATION *(Expand Each Idea. Flesh It Out)*	CLARIFICATION *(Understand The Full Idea)*

Take the list of ideas you are going to work with and write each idea in a section of the IDEA column. Write each idea as it was expressed, taking the ideas in order from the original list of all ideas.

List them all, or if you have used one of the preliminary weeding out strategies, take the remaining ideas and list them all.

Then focus your attention on the first idea and fill in as much as you can to fully clarify what the idea means. Make this meaning as specific as possible. This process of clarification can also involve elaboration as the meaning of an idea is expanded. Once it seems that the idea has been understood to this point, move to the elaboration column and write in more aspects that further expand the idea, or extend how the idea would solve the problem.

Add to the idea as you flesh out how this could be a solution to the problem. Try to make each idea a possible solution. Describe how the idea would work. Look for ways to make the idea better than it first appeared by making the idea, no matter how fantastical, as practical as possible. Link or merge an idea with another if it seems like the two compliment each other.

The objective in this step is to both clarify each idea and to give each idea as much chance to look like the right solution as you can. Forcing yourself to consider each idea as a viable solution and considering how this would work will expand your thinking. Problem-solving optimism grows as more and more ideas are clarified and expanded. This is particularly valuable when a problem is seen as impossible to solve.

As you do this, you enhance your ability to merge solution ideas and to step sideways to consider ideas that might have originally been rejected. As the ideas take on a viable life, the problem-solver expands his or her options.

The process can easily frustrate people who are unused to such thinking. For them it may seem tedious, thinking it belabors work on weak ideas. If such resistance can be set aside, continuous use of this technique will reveal that ideas that might have been rejected can in fact turn out to be the best ideas once they have been clarified and elaborated upon.

If the problem-solver is a group or couple, each member is encouraged to set aside loyalty to any one idea and consider all ideas as viable. The group or couple works together in pursuit of optimum ideas, not to get their own solution selected. This stretches the problem-solver's mind, opening up his or her thinking to new possibilities. It is in this frame of mind that the creativity light bulbs are turned on.

By working in this way, the problem-solver opens up to finding the unusual idea(s) that, once clarified and elaborated, stand out as optimum solutions. These are often ideas that wouldn't have been considered in normal thinking about problems. A creative solution is one that is obvious once seen, but one that wouldn't normally have been discovered.

If the problem is one that is perceived as quite solvable, fewer ideas will be clarified and expanded and the list fleshed out quickly. However, if the problem is seen as almost impossible, then the list of ideas will be longer and more time to clarify and expand ideas will be required. Take the time necessary to go through all of the ideas, even if early on an idea appears after elaboration and clarification to be a satisfactory solution. Avoid making that selection at this stage.

Techniques For Elaboration And Clarification

There are various techniques that can be used to more effectively elaborate and clarify your solution ideas.

GUESS AT MEANING

One way to expand an idea is to allow yourself to guess at the many possible meanings of the idea. This is particularly useful when the problem-solver is more than one person. If all participants look for different possible meanings for a recorded idea, the idea grows and new ways of looking at the idea emerge. In addition, all participants start to take shared ownership of the idea. This shared ownership significantly reduces the chances that a good idea will be prematurely discarded.

Record all guesses. We don't have to arrive at one meaning for the idea. Again, the more possibilities the problem-solver identifies as possible meanings, the better chance that an optimum idea will suddenly emerge.

HITCHHIKING

Hitchhiking is one useful technique for elaborating on ideas and amounts to saying, "This idea is a good one and it will take us even further if we add *this and that* to it." It is the process of thinking of ideas in terms of the idea plus any additions that might make it even better. Search for ways to improve what is already contained in the idea.

For example in looking at ways to make it easier to pick apples, one of the solution ideas might have been "grow them lower to the ground". We can follow a hitchhiking progression like:

- Raise the ground level around the perimeter of the tree.

- Plant the trees between platforms that can be raised or lowered,

- Extend and stretch wire mesh under the branches and trail the branches as they grow so they are all at one height in order to have the fruit hang through to be easily picked,

- Plant the trees in deep rows between two berms in order to get the apples to hang at ground level.

(Note: This is presented only as an example of hitchhiking. I hold no presumption that these ideas are workable, optimum, or even creative solutions for use in apple orchards.)

In dealing with your own problems, hitchhike to make ideas even better by adding elements not originally expressed during the brainstorm. If the problem-solver is a couple or group, hitchhiking furthers cooperation, builds a climate of working together and reduces competition to get one's own idea chosen.

VISUALIZATION

To elaborate on ideas, don't just list them. Freehand draw them. This is akin to drawing ideas out on paper napkins when at lunch. Allow your mind(s) to better understand ideas and to see new possibilities by visualizing them and drawing them out. Sketch without worrying about the quality of the drawing. Just illustrate the idea and any ways to enhance it. If more than one person is problem-solving, share the pen. Encourage additions to the drawing by asking, "What else could we do to make this idea even better?" In our apple orchard example, ideas might be clarified with a drawing something like the following:

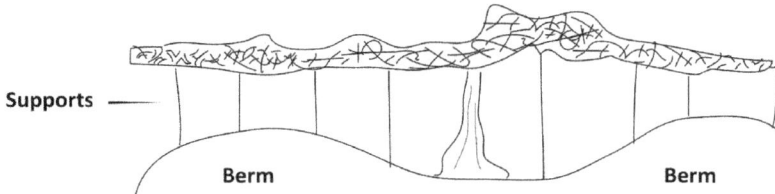

MATCHMAKE IDEAS

Sometimes the quality of a given idea increases when we add it to another idea, even though that idea was generated as a separate possibility. Your list may have an idea that could match and complement another idea. By reading over the brainstormed list, the problem-solver sees ideas that could be naturally grouped together.

As the problem-solver progresses through the entire list, some ideas fall into a category of their own, while other ideas are discovered as ideas that can be connected. The joined ideas might become a viable solution – "We could do this, this and this and get great results." By pooling what several ideas offer, the problem-solver may in fact identify an optimum solution.

For example, in one situation a retail grocer had somehow upset some of the government departments responsible for the retail food industry and he was being subjected to an inordinate amount of inspections, audits and license challenges. In brainstorming, he generated two separate ideas:

- Send a letter facetiously inviting related government departments to re-inspect his facility, and

- Declare in a public notice in the local newspaper that his business was being subjected to undue harassment.

Both of these ideas were obviously expressions of his frustration. In bringing these two ideas together during the process of elaboration, he arrived at:

"Send letters to many respective departments thanking them for the frequent inspections because they were helping to keep the quality of his business up, providing an incentive for his personnel to reduce any mistakes and to provide exceptional service to customers. He could then use these letters in his advertising campaigns, printing the letter in the ad, and saying that his organization strongly believed in the value of government inspection to insure quality for the consumer and that he was proud his outlet had passed more inspections than any other comparable outlets."

Whether this idea will be chosen as his optimum solution or not doesn't matter at this stage. What matters is turning all ideas into possible solutions that could work.

TAKE BREAKS

If you find yourself tiring, stop. Take a break from this step, and do something else. Return when you have the energy to give your enthusiastic attention to each idea. You want this to be an exciting and fun activity. The more impossible the problem is seen to be, the more you should allow yourself to take such breaks.

In your quiet moments, you'll find yourself reflecting on ideas that have already been elaborated and clarified, and new insights about them will emerge. When you return to the task of elaboration, add these thoughts to already covered ideas before proceeding to new items on the list.

RE-INTERPRETATION

One very useful technique is to look at the words used when the idea was first presented and interpret the meaning of the words in different ways. Find other meanings for the words in order to uncover useful alternative elements of the idea.

For example, a group of student nurses who were extremely taxed by the demands of their newly designed educational program were elaborating, to much laughter, one of the ideas that had been expressed during the brainstorm – "put more fibre in their diet by cutting up a particularly large and troublesome text book into shreds and eating it." Via re-interpretation, this idea became "divide the book up into easily digestible chunks and assign different chunks to different individuals who will then read and extract the meat of their section then share the summary with the whole group."

In another example where a group was brainstorming uses for a 36" piece of 1/16th inch wire, someone said "snake beater" and everyone laughed. Later when in this step and elaborating this idea, the group moved from snake beater to whip to egg whip, thereby producing a practical solution to the problem. Looked at more closely this process produced a viable solution possibility with real market value from an idea that all members originally considered to be funny and useless.

SEVEN EXAGGERATIONS

One method of elaboration involves developing seven exaggerations for each idea. An exaggeration is a magnification of an idea beyond the limits of truth by:

- enlarging the scope or range of an idea,

- emphasizing one particular aspect of an idea and blowing it up to a grand scale,

- promising that an idea would lead to an outcome that might at first appear to be impossible,

- telling tall tales about the use of the idea,

- making up reasons why the idea is the best idea, or

- adding more and more dimension to an idea to enlarge it.

However, this technique does demand more elaboration of ideas than most other methods because it specifies seven exaggerations for each idea. The technique is most useful in problem situations where there is either a high potential payoff involved or where a solution is initially regarded as impossible.

To use this technique, the problem-solver needs to relax and set aside his or her internal critic and freely fantasize about one idea until seven different exaggerations or extensions of the idea have emerged. This mini brainstorm requires the willingness to consider new and fantastical ideas as possible. Dupont USA, in their research into creativity, found that this willingness to consider new ideas as possible even when commonly regarded as impossible led to significant breakthroughs in the development of new products.

When To Move To The Next Stage

Once all ideas have been clarified, and best efforts have been made to:

- elaborate and expand each idea,
- group ideas that compliment each other to create workable solutions, and
- find all of the best attributes of each idea,

it's time to move to the next step. A decision as to which idea is the best solution should not yet have been made.

If the problem-solver is already narrowing his or her attention to one particular idea or solution, then go back. Re-examine at least three other ideas and make them the best that you can so they truly do compare favorably with the idea that seems to be pre-empting the problem-solver's attention. Force yourself into a situation where you will have to decide between several possible optimum solutions.

You'll know it's time to move on when you have elaborated and clarified each of the ideas in your original list; or, if you purged some of them to have a more manageable list to work with, when you have expanded and better understand all ideas on the shorter list. Do not move forward until all ideas have been fully clarified, enhanced and turned as closely as they can be into fully developed ideas that could work.

Transition To The Next Stage

To move forward, the problem-solver needs to think to him or her self, or if the problem-solver is a group, someone needs to say,

"Well we now have some solidly fleshed out ideas that provide at least several workable solution options. It's almost time to move forward to selecting our solution, but before we do, we need to take a break. We've worked hard to get here and tried our best to let creative ideas emerge. For now, stop thinking about the problem and just engage with play, music, reading or some other work issue. How long do you think we need to break for?"

or

"Great, we have a fantastic list of clarified and expanded potential solutions. We've really exercised our creative thinking muscles so now it's time to rest. Let's take a break until ..."

Step Six:
Take A Break

It takes work to move from a comfort with the status quo to being ready to make a significant change. The problem-solver's mind is in a state of turmoil as he or she searches for all of the elements of the problem, sorts through what he or she would really like to achieve, storms through the process of generating many possible solutions, then works at turning each idea into a mature, well thought-out solution possibility. When done properly, this is a fidgety process with lots of nervous energy and a great deal of enjoyment and excitement. The second half is going to involve a different type of energy – one of critical judgement, evaluation, exclusion and selection. To make the mental shift to prepare for critical thinking, it's time for a break.

Insight Potential When "Taking A Break" – *During the lull in problem-solving, and while the problem-solver is distracted with other things, new ideas can emerge from the problem-solver's subconscious mind. These ideas might form optimum solutions. Alternatively, the problem-solver might find him or herself focussing on one particular solution possibility that emerged in this first half, feeling the excitement that a solution may have emerged.*

To this stage, you have creatively developed your understanding of the full problem, and produced many potential solution options. This took work even though it was fun if you used the creative processes identified in the earlier chapters. Now it's time to set aside the work.

The problem has certainly not yet been solved but you've made a lot of progress. It's time to take a break – five to twenty minutes, four to five hours, or one to seven days depending on how significant and complex your problem is.

It's time to shift to thinking and working on something completely different. You might have an insignificant item on your "To Do" list that you could tackle and complete before returning to your work on this problem. Or you may have to go back to your day-to-day work and wait until a meeting can be set up to pursue the second half of your problem-solving process.

Set your prior work on the specific problem aside and focus on something else. Let the information that emerged in the first five steps percolate in your subconscious mind. The creative process is not quite done. By taking time to separate yourself from the work you've already done, by focussing on something totally unrelated to the problem(s), you give yourself a chance to allow an unfettered, uncontrolled subconscious to poke new ideas up into your conscious thinking.

Your break will have to be shorter if your deadline for having a solution in place is rapidly approaching, but then it should be much more intense. Use a technique that truly pulls your conscious attention away from the problem and forces you to think of something completely different, and maybe even at a different pace. For example, choose an activity that gets your adrenaline and bodily juices flowing, or engage in some activity that generates lots of laughter.

Goals Of The "Take A Break" Step

It may appear that you've stopped work on the problem during this step because you're doing other things. However, you haven't because your subconscious mind is still at work and you still have several problem-solving goals to achieve:

- Quiet your mind somewhat by stopping the fidgety, open ended, and creative thinking that you have been overtly doing in the first half.

- Let the information you have already brought to the surface percolate within your subconscious thought processes so that new associations can be made.

- Allow your mind to send other ideas to your conscious attention through dreams, distracted thoughts as you focus on something else, or through perception of connections you had not made before.

- Take a rest from the intensity of the first half of the problem-solving process.

and

- Finish off your creative open-ended thinking and prepare for a shift to structured, judgmental, evaluative and exclusion-oriented thinking.

This is a period of consciously doing nothing associated with the problem. However, your subconscious doesn't take the break in the same way. It works below your awareness to make new associations, to make connections to past experiences, to perceive the problem in different ways. Once such connections are made, clues are forced up into your conscious awareness through your dreams, fantasies, or sudden hunches.

Match Your Break Period To The Complexity Of Your Problem

Some problems are small enough that the process of sorting through the S.P.I.C.E[3] then generating solution possibilities and elaborating on each possibility can be completed very quickly. Some problems are much more complex, and much more significant to the problem-solver with high costs of failure if the problem is not solved, and high payoffs if an optimum solution is produced.

A general principle to follow is to make the length of the break match the difficulty and significance of the problem. Smaller, less significant problems don't need much of a break because it didn't take all that much effort to complete the first five steps. However, problems that have high stakes will take longer to define and require much more creative intensity in identifying possible solutions. Take more time when the problem is both more difficult and more significant.

Difficulty And Significance Of The Problem	Duration Of The Break
Simple problem of minor or moderate significance to the problem-solver that takes five to twenty minutes to define, generate solution possibilities and then elaborate on each idea.	5-20 minutes
Moderate problem that takes two to four hours to complete the first five steps.	2-4 hours or up to 1 day
More complex problem that is perceived to be very difficult and of serious significance to the problem-solver, taking up to a day or a couple of separate meetings to work through the first five steps of the problem-solving process.	1 to 2 days
Very complex problem that is believed to be almost impossible to solve and is very significant to the problem-solver, taking multiple meetings to define, generate solution possibilities, and to elaborate on each idea.	5-7 days from completing the first half of the problem-solving process.

Set a definite time for your break and stick to it. Arrange for an alarm or reminder to let you know when time is up. Allow your conscious mind to take a break from the problem, but your subconscious processes will likely continue to percolate for the whole break period.

Techniques For The "Take A Break" Step

There are various ways you can enhance your problem-solving work even while taking a break. Make a deliberate decision as to which of these techniques you will adopt for your particular problem.

Ideally, what you choose to do will take your conscious mind completely off the problem. In addition, any change of emotion between what you felt as you worked through the first five steps is better than doing something that feels the same way. If you can involve laughter during your break, even better as laughter really will distract the conscious mind and allow new associations to emerge.

- **Watch Funny Videos** - Don't look for anything related to your problem. Just look for something you might find to be a potentially funny topic and click and watch.

- **Tell Jokes** - If the problem-solver is more than one person, stop the discussion of the problem and just start telling each other jokes that have nothing to do with the problem.

- **Tell Stories** -Take a few minutes and just tell a story that might induce some degree of emotion – sadness, anger, disbelief, surprise, joy, exasperation – in the listener.

- **Take A Walk** - Get up and take a walk, possibly just around the building you've been working in for a short break, or for a longer break, over a longer distance to a park, forest or open field. Notice any wild life or natural elements around you.

- **Meditate** - Find a comfortable place to sit upright, take four deep breaths, and then meditate for twenty minutes letting your mind go still. Just let any thoughts pass on through your mind, and without any tension, just bring your awareness back to your breathing.

- **Tackle Your "TO DO" List** - Make a list of all the tasks and jobs that need to be done that have nothing to do with the problem, prioritize according to each task's do-ability during the break period, then tackle these chores with a vengeance.

- **Spend Time With Family And Friends** – to maximize your distraction, spend the break time socializing with people that have nothing to do with the problem, and if possible, spend time just playing with children.

- **Go To A Movie** - Go to a movie theater to watch a movie that has nothing to do with your problem, and immerse yourself into the fantasy of the movie you are watching.

- **Read A Book** - Find a novel or fact based book that has nothing to do with your problem situation and read.

- **Engage In Intense Play Or Physical Work** – Go play racquet ball, tennis, hockey, pickle ball, flag football, slow-pitch or do some other relatively intense activity – swim, run, lift weights, chop wood, skip rope, wall climb, etc.

- **Record Problem Related Ideas** - Carry a small notepad or your smartphone and if any ideas related to your problem surface during the break, record the ideas when they emerge.

When To Move To The Next Step

It will only be time to transition to the next step when you have completed the time frame for the break that you set at the beginning of this step. It is inappropriate to cut the break short, or to prolong the break beyond the planned period.

Don't stop early just because you surfaced a new idea or piece of information that excites you. You can record the idea and return to the non-problem-solving activity. You may be tempted to get back to the problem sooner than the scheduled return time, but avoid doing so.

Alternatively, you might find yourself resisting a return to problem-solving. Contemplate that resistance to see if you can identify what it's about. Perhaps your subconscious mind realizes that you haven't really completed some aspect of the first steps and need to return to do so. Sometimes the other activities can become so engaging, or so distracting that they draw the problem-solver away from the problem. This is likeliest if the problem is perceived as too difficult to solve, or alternatively, too insignificant to solve. Once you've pondered the question, "What is my resistance about?", return to your problem-solving site and continue your problem-solving work.

Before you move to the next step, write down any information or ideas that surfaced during the break period. Write them down as completely as you can, organized as part of the S.P.I.C.E[3], or part of the list of possible solutions, or as part of the elaboration of a particular idea. You want to include these ideas during the first step of the second half. In the coming step, you will review the written record of the problem and solution possibilities that you produced in the first half. Any ideas that merged during the break should be written down before you start that step.

You've set a time frame for your break so stick to it and get ready to move to the next step when your break time has expired.

Transition To The Next Stage

To make the transition, the problem-solver needs to make a mental shift to get back to working on the problem. Hopefully an alarm will sound to notify you that the break is over, or a meeting reminder will appear in your electronic calendar.

The problem-solver needs to think to him or herself, or if the problem-solver is more than one participant, someone needs to say something like,

"Okay, break time is over. Does anyone have any new ideas or information that needs to be recorded on our work sheets?"

If the answer is "yes" get the person with the idea to write it down on the viewable sheets or whiteboard and to explain what it means to him or her. If any other person has anything to add to that idea, get that recorded as well. Do this until all ideas that emerged during the break have been recorded, clarified and elaborated. Once done, then the problem-solver needs to think or say,

"We're now shifting to the second half of the problem-solving sequence. In this half, we put on our critical thinking cap and get ready to make a decision. It's time to focus on which idea or set of ideas is the optimal alternative to generate the expectations, desired benefits and improved results we specified in our problem definition. First, we have to review the material we generated in the first half?"

114

The Second Half – RELAX

You're now going to use the normal human impulse to organize, to find structure, to make critical judgments that narrow down the options and give a direct path to the solution. During the creative thinking of the first half, you provided some organization by keeping a written record of the information and ideas that you considered. You will now use that as the material to evaluate and from which you will select a workable solution. There are five steps to the second half.

Review the information

Evaluate each of the ideas

Lock Onto The Optimum Solution(s)

Action Plan

eXecute

In the first half of the problem-solving sequence, we try to maximize our creative thinking, holding an open mind to any information, considering it all relevant and treating all solution possibilities as potentially the optimum solution. That thinking process can be highly energized, even frenetic. It can even be fun because we open our minds to the fantastical.

In the second half, we become more judgmental. Our goal is to weed out the ideas that don't have merit as the best possible solution. It's now time to get critical of these ideas, to put them to a real test:

- Is the idea logical enough to work?

- Are there any inherent downsides or negative attributes to this idea that will bring about costs we don't want, either now or later as time passes?

- Can we afford to implement the idea or would it cost more than we can bear?

- Do we have the necessary resources to make this solution work (people, money, space, equipment, etc.)?

- Is any other idea a better solution, less costly to implement, more acceptable to those who will be impacted, and with better potential results?

- Will this idea overcome any of the real constraints and roadblocks that we identified?

- Will we be able to fully implement this solution by our deadline?

- Will the idea do what we want (get the full set of desired benefits)?

- Does this solution fit within a group of solutions that when working together, can exceed our expectations and desired benefits?

This requires deliberate thinking most commonly associated with conscious brain activity. Using the functions of our conscious mind, we organize, evaluate, think critically, form comparisons, determine "better-thans", and make decisions.

Where creative thinking can be "fidgety" or frenetic, bouncing around without borders or limits, critical thinking is much more structured, focussed and deliberate. Because the pace of critical thinking is usually calmer, this second half is associated with the word – RELAX. Settle in and work through the material to arrive at a choice of the best solution or set of solutions, plan how they will be implemented, and get them executed so that you have a solved problem. Certainly, once you have your optimum solution(s) in place, you can relax into your new status quo.

When the problem-solver is more than one person, many people associate this second half with conflict and disagreement. In typical problem-solving behavior, only a few ideas are offered, discussed, and then argued over to try to make a decision that people will accept. This can involve a lot of conflict and tension when the participants aren't cooperating and hold passionate commitments to one of the ideas.

However, if you followed this problem-solving model, then the cooperation that you established in the first half will make this second half easier and calmer. You will have established a norm of cooperating, listening to each other, and respecting what each participant has to offer. In addition, the amount of ideas that you considered means that there is far greater likelihood that the optimum solution(s) will be obvious to all involved.

So in this second half, relax knowing that you have at least several possible solutions that can achieve your desired outcome. You don't have to focus on just picking an acceptable solution – you have the luxury of picking from amongst several quite viable alternatives and quite possibly a set of solutions that can achieve results beyond your initial expectations. You have a real opportunity to pick the best solution(s).

Step Seven: Review

Review what has been written down. If during this process, new ideas or information surfaces, write it in the appropriate section. Generally, this will be the end of the creative process. Before moving forward, each problem-solver needs to be reminded what was considered in the first half so the deliberation that follows is directed at solving the same problem. Each person must be on the same page.

Insight Potential During The "Review" Step – *The problem-solver might come to see the problem differently because of the combination of taking a break and this review. Such perceptual shifts can add clarity, provide a realization that something is more important than first considered, give a whole new meaning to a piece of information or idea, or add an urgency to finding a solution.*

In this step, review the information in order to remind yourself of the problem definition, the solution possibilities and most specifically what you are trying to achieve.

Goals Of The Review Step

During this step, provide space for the last remnants of the creative thinking process and then bring about a distinct shift to a more critical type of thinking. Your goals at this stage are to:

- Review everything that is understood about the S.P.I.C.E[3] so the problem-solver understands the gap between where the problem-solver is now and where the problem-solver wants to be, what it costs to not have the problem solved just yet, what stops progress in that direction, and the exciting and desirable benefits and gains that could be realized if a new solution is found.

- Review all of the solution possibilities and the elaborations of each idea to fully see the range of different options that have been generated so far.

- Allow any new ideas and information to be added to the problem-solver's understanding of the problem and list of solution options.

- Allow your subconscious mind to send other ideas to your conscious attention.

and

- Finish off your creative open-ended thinking and prepare for a shift to structured, judgmental, evaluative and exclusion-oriented thinking.

Technique For Effective Review

Make sure that your written record of the information and ideas generated in the first half is readily viewable by the problem-solver. If that material was written on flip chart paper, post all of the sheets around the room. If written on notepaper by a single problem-solver, have those notes readily viewable in an organized fashion. If the material was transcribed to a computer file, then project that file onto a wall or screen so all participants can review it.

One participant would then start by reviewing the notes on the situation, then the problem(s), then the implications, then the constraints and finally the goal (the E^3 results) including the problem-solver's expectations, most desirable benefits, and degree of eagerness to get this problem solved. If there is more than one problem-solving participant, another person could then review each solution idea along with all notes of clarification and elaboration so that the remaining problem-solvers know and understand the complete solution possibilities.

Once the review has been completed, the problem-solver should ask:

- Is the problem definition (S.P.I.C.E^3) clear and complete?

- Is there still agreement that this problem needs to be solved?

- Is each solution possibility as completely described as it can be?

- Is each solution possibility fully understood?

If these questions bring up any concerns, confusions, or additional questions, discuss them and get to the place where the problem-solver is ready to proceed.

When To Move To The Next Step

If the answers to these questions are all "YES", then the problem-solver would move to the next step. If not, then further work needs to be done until the answers are "YES".

If the problem-solver is one person, then he or she must have a clear understanding of the gap between what he or she has and what he or she wants, and all of the elements that reside within that gap. If the problem-solver is more than one person, then all participants must have a shared understanding of the problem so they can effectively evaluate the ability of each solution possibility to achieve the desired outcomes.

Transition To The Evaluation Step

When the problem definition is fully understood and the solution possibilities have been sufficiently elaborated, the problem-solver would then declare,

"It's now time to put each solution possibility to the test – will it achieve the desired outcomes with the resources that we have available within the deadline period that we require?"

This means examining each of the solution possibilities fairly and in the same way. So the individual problem-solver would ask him or her self,

"Which method of evaluation seems most appropriate for this problem?"

Where more than one problem-solver is involved, then some agreement must be reached as to which technique will be used. One of the participants must ask,

"We have different techniques we could use to evaluate our ideas. Does anyone think a particular technique would work best for this problem?"

Step Eight: Evaluation

Up to now, the problem-solver has suspended his or her critical thinking while focussing on more creative processes. It is now time to make a shift to more organized, structured, critical, judgmental, evaluative thinking. The problem-solver has generated many solution possibilities and must now consider whether or not the possibilities will deliver what is wanted and which of them are the best possible solutions.

Insight Potential When "Evaluating" – *By using structured processes to fairly evaluate each idea against the same criteria, an idea might emerge as a best possible solution when it might have originally been discarded. In turn, what might have first appeared as a workable solution might be discovered wanting in a key manner that means the solution can't produce the desired outcomes within the deadline. Surprises can result as the ideas are all compared against the same requirements. By treating all ideas in the same way, by evaluating all ideas against the same criteria, it is possible that you will surprise yourself when you discover which idea produces the best benefits with the least cost of implementation.*

Hopefully, this step involves the first appearance of any critical thinking or negative assessment of the ideas that were generated as possible solutions. Everything should have been done to prevent such criticism and evaluation before this moment. However, it's now time to open the door to judgmental thinking. But, this step still does not involve selection of a solution. That will come later.

Before this point in time, we wanted to treat each idea as a viable solution so that each idea had the opportunity to receive fair consideration and to be fully understood and expanded. Please note – that objective remains. Even as we enter into the critical evaluation process, we still want to give creative ideas an opportunity to emerge as optimum solutions.

Goals Of Evaluation

This step does not involve making a decision. It is the step to prepare for one, and the goals include:

- Fairly evaluate all ideas.

- Identify all of the strengths, advantages, benefits of each idea before considering any negatives, weaknesses, and costs.

- Continue to expand on ideas by adding not yet considered elements that might surface during the evaluation phase.

- Compare all ideas with the same measures.

- Use measures that match your primary decision criteria – what must each idea satisfy to be considered an optimum solution?

and

- Minimize conflicts, which usually occur when there is a fight or argument over which idea is better, either within the problem-solver's mind or between problem-solving participants.

Having clarified and expanded most, if not all, of the ideas that emerged in brainstorming, we have a large pool of possible solutions to consider. Now we can put on our analytic hats and evaluate each of the ideas to get a measure of the potential payoffs, and costs of implementing such ideas. At this stage, each idea must now demonstrate that it is the best possible solution.

The objective of this step is to determine the strengths and weaknesses, advantages and disadvantages, and potential payoffs and costs of each idea. Once again, the actual selection of the solution to be implemented is delayed until a later step. A decision will be made but not now.

Rules For Effective Evaluation

This model holds to certain beliefs:

- that many ideas are better than a few,

- that clarifying and expanding ideas is better than fighting over the righteousness of them,

- that looking for the positives about each idea first is better than "knocking all of the stuffing out of an idea then trying to find something good about it."

- that all ideas should be measured against the same criteria.

Consequently, within this model, there are specific rules to be followed when evaluating your solution ideas.

1. Positives First

Because the norm in typical problem-solving has been to criticize ideas first and because this kills creativity, it's best to work with the "positives first" rule in any of the evaluation methods used. This rule limits the problem-solver to identifying positive values of an idea before any negative criticism can be expressed. If the problem-solver, or any member of a problem-solving group or couple, has already formed preferences, this rule can be unsettling.

If a problem-solver forces him or herself to identify the positives of each idea despite having a preference, then it is harder to hang on to only one idea as the best idea. As potential advantages are explored for other ideas, particularly when they were previously out of favor, the problem-solver's awareness opens up to potential benefits of such ideas. His or her tight grasp on only one solution is loosened and there is room for new and better possibilities to surface.

2. Record Everything

Gather and organize the information that you generate about the benefits and disadvantages. Record and keep track of all the information that is developed. Keep the information visible. Develop charts that can be posted on the walls, a blackboard, an electronic whiteboard, or flip chart where the information can be seen and compared at a glance.

If the problem-solver is an individual, this process of recording retains the information so the problem-solver doesn't have to worry about considering too many ideas and forgetting good ones. If the problem-solver is a couple or group, recording all of the information rewards each contributor by including their information in the pool of data that will be considered in the next step.

Keeping track of this information provides a back-up source of information to use if the problem solution has to be justified to others. For example, a problem-solving group at work can demonstrate to superiors, or other people who will be impacted by a solution, that many ideas were thoroughly considered and the chosen solution rose to the top because of the recorded reasons. This can win wider support for the solution and increase chances of success.

3. Record Without Editing

The person who records the information should be instructed to write down what has been said as it has been said. The Recorder should not be allowed to change the wording. If the Recorder wants a shorter version to write down, the person offering the information could be asked to rephrase the information in a more concise form, and that would then be what is written down.

4. Look For The Agreements

In general, adopt the attitude that all information has value. However, if participants think a piece of information is incorrect, the objective is to find value in the information and not get into conflict. Discuss the information considering its validity from all perspectives and find where the participants can agree as to the usefulness of the information. Work together. Don't put the participant that offered the information into a position where he or she must defend it. Look for the agreements in any disputes.

Discuss cooperatively, looking for ways to use the information. If after discussion there is a consensus that the information is not accurate, then it can be modified or discarded but all participants should feel this is the correct action to take.

5. Agree On The Evaluation Criteria First

All ideas are to be evaluated using the same criteria. The criteria should directly relate to the intended outcomes (the E^3 results). If working as a couple or a group, all participants should agree on what the criteria are to be. If an individual problem-solver, he or she should decide, in advance, what criteria will be used to evaluate each of the ideas. All ideas should be treated equally. This is done to prevent one person, when working in a couple or group, from lobbying for a particular idea, or to prevent the individual problem-solver from locking on to one idea too soon.

Techniques For Improving Problem-Solving At The Evaluation Step

There are several ways to organize your work at this step. Pick an approach that seems to best fit the nature of the problem on which you are working. Less difficult problems or those that aren't seen as high-payoff problems can use simple evaluation techniques that involve an assessment of the positives and negatives of each idea. More complex problems, or those seen as almost impossible to solve, or those where significant gains could be realized, should involve more deliberate and thorough evaluation processes.

DEFINE THE MEASUREMENT CRITERIA

Make a list of what these criteria are to be. If necessary, clarify any that someone does not understand. Arrive at an agreement that the identified criteria, and only the identified criteria, are to be used.

If during the evaluation process, the problem-solver starts to introduce a new criterion when evaluating one idea, notice this, then discuss whether it should be added to the list. If so, go back and evaluate all previously discussed ideas using that criterion as well.

THE PAYOFF/COST APPROACH

This is a very commonly used and simple evaluation technique that can be used quickly. Please notice that the usual order of words to delineate this approach has been reversed from Cost/Payoff to satisfy our rule to consider positive attributes first. The technique involves making two lists for each idea.

One lists the potential payoffs. A payoff is some possible gain to be achieved by using the idea. List as many of these potential gains as you can. A gain is any potential benefit that would be produced by implementing the idea and that could be financial, emotional, relationship based, or other intangible results.

The second list involves identifying or predicting the costs associated with an idea. A cost could be any expenditure required to implement an idea, any negative impacts on any person or aspect of the problem situation, or any losses that might result. Expenditures could be measured in terms of emotion, effort, resources, or actual dollar costs that would be consumed to make the idea work.

Complete the payoffs list first because it is too easy to think of negatives and prematurely reject ideas because the payoffs weren't fairly considered. By thinking of positives first, each idea is more effectively considered. After the payoffs and costs have been considered for each idea, the problem-solver will have a sense of which ideas have the best payoffs at the least cost.

THE ADVANTAGES/DISADVANTAGES (PRO'S/CON'S) APPROACH

This technique is similar to the Payoff/Cost approach in that two lists are built for each idea. The problem-solver brainstorms what might be the advantages of the idea and then what might be the disadvantages. Do this for every idea before identifying which ideas are best. On completion, the problem-solver will have the best sense of which ideas are stronger solutions.

THE PROJECTED RESULTS APPROACH

One useful technique for evaluation involves an imagined projection into the future to guess at the consequences that might be experienced by implementing each idea. It is useful to make three lists of anticipated results.

One list specifies the results to be experienced immediately upon implementation. The second list can focus on those short-term results that might be expected in the follow-up period after the immediate consequences of implementation. For example, if the immediate period is decided to be from 0 – 6 months after implementation, then the short-term period could be 6 months to 3 years. The third list is then used to identify those consequences that might be predicted over a longer period of time (for example, 3 years or more).

To populate the lists, brainstorm what the problem-solver thinks might happen without questioning, challenging, or critiquing the guessed outcomes. The objective is to think forward and anticipate both the benefits and what could go wrong once the solution has been implemented.

Sometimes we fail to identify important consequences because we focus exclusively on the more immediate excitement of getting the problem solved. This produces two types of error. Type one errors occur when an idea is rejected because we fail to see its long run payoffs. We make this mistake when we place a much higher value on the changes to be gained immediately. Type two errors occur when an idea is accepted without realizing its potential negative effects over time.

Type I - Error of OMISSION	Failing to do something that would have produced the best possible results.
Type II - Error Of COMMISSION	Doing something that resulted in negative consequences that hadn't been considered before taking action.

This technique is a deliberate attempt to prevent either type of error. Doing this structures our thinking so we are more likely to project accurately into the future and foresee possible consequences for each idea. This sensitizes the problem-solver to what must be done to achieve a successful implementation of the solution that has the most promise.

"PAN"NING IDEAS

One useful technique involves a melding of the elaboration and evaluation steps together by PANning each idea. This stands for the process of making three different lists for each solution possibility:

- Positives
- Additions or extensions
- Negatives

In one list, specify as many positive attributes as you can for the given idea. This would include estimates of the benefits such as increased revenues, reduced costs, improved results, intangible benefits, positive impact on others, and rewards to be achieved. In the second list, specify any additions or extensions you could make to enhance or further develop the solution idea. In the third list, specify all of the negative aspects of the idea that remain once the idea has been expanded. This would include cost estimates, lower potential results compared to potential results from other solutions, negative impacts on others, or anticipated disadvantages.

This process will trigger useful changes that increase the sophistication and appropriateness of an idea as a solution. The sequence of looking at positives first then the additions forces an orientation toward valuing all ideas and looking for ways to build on rather than tear down ideas. Each list can be brainstormed to insure that the problem-solver loosens up and lets him or herself develop an orientation for expansion of basic ideas before having to get serious to look for the weaknesses or difficulties of each idea.

FORMAL EVALUATION REPORT

In a business setting, individuals or teams could prepare formal reports identifying the predicted financial costs and benefits, the human resource implications, impacts on organizational assets, any intangible costs or benefits that might result from the implementation of each idea. Using the same criteria, individuals or small teams could be assigned a specific solution possibility, research the potential gains and costs of implementing that idea, and then write a report on their conclusions. The whole group could then come together and review the reports to prepare to make a decision.

An individual or couple could do the same thing for any life change or significant problem such as retirement planning, career change, geographical relocation, change in marital status or family size, or possible vacation and leisure activities. By explicitly conducting this research and writing it down, the best ideas become more obvious.

MATRIX EVALUATION

In difficult or high cost/payoff situations, it's helpful to use a method that involves the building of a comprehensive matrix. A matrix is a graphic method of organizing and illustrating information. Used in this step, the matrix organizes as much information as possible about the values of each solution alternative.

The major function of a matrix is to organize evaluative information in such a way that the optimum solution can be identified at a glance. The secondary function of using a matrix is to further inhibit the preference formation process before all ideas have been fully considered.

Set up a matrix before any evaluation is done and then proceed to evaluate every idea within the matrix against all of the criteria in the matrix:

1. List all of the important considerations, criteria, and consequences that the problem-solver might use to evaluate any idea. These are the decision criteria the problem-solver will use to make a selection of a solution for this problem. For example, the decision criteria might include cost, expected payoff, the expected results, convenience, time requirements, resources required, impact on others, comfort, etc.

2. Prioritize the decision criteria according to the value system of the problem-solver. For example, the criteria can be sorted into groups such as absolutely necessary, highly desired, somewhat desired, optional, and frills; or simply grouped as high, medium and low priorities. If the problem-solver is a group or couple,

this discussion must result in a ranking for each item that satisfies all participants.

3. Down the left hand side of the matrix, list the expanded ideas. Across the top of the matrix, write the criteria in their priority groups. This allows the lining off of information you will need in order to evaluate all ideas against all of the criteria.

4. Evaluate each alternative idea, as objectively as possible, against each of the criteria. Seek out missing information in order to complete the matrix and fairly evaluate each idea.

5. Looking at all of the information that has been filled in the boxes in the matrix, rank each idea based on how well each idea has satisfied all of the criteria. More weight would be given to the more important criteria.

For example:

Criteria

Solution Ideas	Essential			Desired				Optional			Overall Rank
	Cr #1	Cr #2	Cr #3	Cr #4	Cr #5	Cr #6	Cr #7	Cr #8	Cr #9	Cr #10	
A											
B											
C											
D											
E											
F											
G											
H											

Solution Ideas Are Written Out In Their Clarified And Expanded Form

The matrix evaluation procedure is much more complex and has its own payoffs and costs that need to be considered in deciding whether or not to use this technique.

Payoffs

1. Surfaces and makes public all of the information pertinent to evaluation.

2. Forces more deliberate research into the potential benefits and costs of each idea.

3. Treats all ideas equally in terms of time given to consideration.

4. Some ideas emerge as better choices on the basis of comparison of all ideas against the same criteria.

5. Allows an arguing over decision criteria without having to argue over ideas, which protects potentially creative and optimal solutions from premature rejection.

6. All members of a problem-solving group are able to make a contribution and be heard.

7. Emphasizes the priority of decision criteria so that ideas are seen as best for the right reasons.

Costs

1. Takes considerable time to complete.

2. Requires an organized effort to sort through a great deal of evaluative information about all ideas.

3. In establishing the decision criteria and the priority of those criteria, differences in values may be identified between members of a problem-solving group and conflict may occur.

4. The matrix tries to separate out opinion from factual information, which forces the problem-solver to dig out as much factual evaluation as possible and suspend preferences expressed as opinions.

5. Requires a search for objective information, which means more work.

6. Inhibits the persuasion model of evaluation and selection, which can frustrate members with already formed strong preferences.

For the matrix evaluation process to work effectively, it's helpful to have a very large viewable area to see all of the information placed in the matrix. Flipchart sheets mounted on a wall could be used or a large black or white board would work. An individual could use a spreadsheet on a computer. A group with a projector attached to a computer could enter information into a spreadsheet and have the screen image projected onto the wall to facilitate full viewership of the information.

Some problem-solvers find this method to be tedious because the rules of matrix evaluation prevent the problem-solver from just making a snap judgment as to which idea is best. Recording all of the information feels like a chore.

Some problem-solvers have tried to simplify and quantify the matrix by entering a rating in each square based on how the problem-solver sees an idea falling on each decision criteria. For example, if the idea is seen as exceptional in a given decision criteria, it would be assigned a 10, and conversely if the idea is seen as very weak, then a 0 or 1 could be assigned. By adding all of the ratings across the line for that idea, a supposed quantifiable result would be shown.

For some situations there is the option of the abbreviated matrix evaluation. Select five to eight ideas that are considered to be most promising based on the problem-solver's general sense of all ideas and then pick at least two additional ideas that are seen as unusual or somewhat fantastical in nature. The problem-solver might have a teasing sense that these two options may have real potential. Working with this shorter list of up to ten ideas in the matrix is much more manageable. However, there is a risk that optimum solutions might be excluded and the problem less than satisfactorily solved.

This is a very complex evaluation process that is likely to be most useful when dealing with very difficult or potentially high-payoff problems. It takes time to complete a full matrix especially when there are many solution ideas and many decision criteria to be considered. However, that's when the potential payoffs justify the work involved.

When the matrix is large, work on completion of the matrix over several sessions. It does not have to be done all in one sitting and makes the time spent more productive because there is less information fatigue. In turn, breaking the evaluation step into two or more sessions makes the completion of a complex matrix much more pleasurable.

When To Move To The Next Step

You will know it's time to move on when you have considered the positive value of each idea first, then identified the negative aspects of each idea, and organized this information in a readily reviewable format. You must have fairly evaluated the pro's and con's of each idea, keeping the full set of evaluation criteria in mind. Whichever technique you've used, you want to really understand the potential benefits for each idea and the potential negative consequences if an idea is implemented.

You can move forward when you know that you have several solution ideas that:

- will achieve the desired E^3 benefits and results,
- do not have any inherent downsides or negative costs you don't want, either now or later as time passes,
- you can afford to implement,
- you have the necessary resources to make each solution work (people, money, space, equipment, etc.),
- will overcome any of the real constraints and roadblocks, and
- can be fully implemented by your deadline.

Do not move forward until all ideas have been fully considered. You should not have made any decisions yet or selected any particular solutions but your process of evaluating ideas should be getting you significantly closer to doing so because that is the next step.

Transition To The Next Step

Upon recognizing that the evaluation step has been completed, the problem-solver can think to him or herself,

"Wow! I now have several really good possibilities to choose from. It's time to make a decision. How shall I choose?"

134

Or if more than one participant is involved, one of the parties needs to say something like,

"Okay, we've reached crunch time. We've comprehensively looked at each idea so now a decision must be made. Is there a decision-making technique that would best fit this problem situation?"

Step Nine:
Lock Onto The Optimum Solution(s)

You now have an abundance of solution possibilities to consider. This is your opportunity to select the best solution or combination of solutions that will yield the optimum results, bring about the desired change, all within the resources that you have available, and by the required deadline. You now go from a broad focus on all possibilities to a narrow focus on those that are the best possible solutions.

Insight Potential When "Locking On" – *The problem-solver may be surprised that a combination of solution possibilities is possible and will yield the best possible outcomes. In turn, the problem-solver may be surprised by what are ultimately selected as the solutions to be put into action. You have the potential of selecting a solution you would not have conceived of before engaging in this process of creative problem-solving but now see as obviously the best solution. In the case where there is more than one problem-solver, you might achieve synergy – arriving at a solution that is better than any single participant could have produced on his or her own.*

Your large pool of solution possibilities has been fully expanded and clarified, then fully evaluated to specify both the positive and negative values of each idea. With all of this information visible in front of you, it's time to select the solution ideas that have the best potential.

Many problem-solvers set out to find one solution to a given problem. By following the preceding steps in the manner that has been described, the problem-solver should be looking at many good options and because of their differences, may see how several of them could be implemented at the same time to really produce exceptional results.

From all of the solution possibilities, select those options that will best close the problem gap between where you are now and where you want to be. Select what will yield the best results at the most acceptable cost, and be implemented with the greatest degree of enthusiasm by the desired or required deadline.

> An idea that appears to be the best idea but won't be implemented well, or on time, is a poor solution.

Goals Of The "Lock On" Step

The ultimate goal is to both select a solution or set of solutions that has the highest probability of resulting in the exciting benefits desired by the problem-solver, and to select a solution or set of solutions that will be eagerly implemented by the deadline by those that must carry out the solution(s). The goals of this step also include arriving at a selection of the optimum solution through a process that is satisfactory to the problem-solver.

- Determine how the decision will be made.

- Identify the optimum solution(s) based on all of the information you gathered and organized.

- Select solutions that yield your desired E^3 outcomes, or if several solutions meet your criteria, then select those that give you the greatest benefits beyond your desired E^3 outcomes.

- When possible, select more than one solution to implement, and if not, select the best one.

- Select solutions that can be and will be successfully implemented before the deadline is reached.

- Select solutions that you can afford to implement given your resources.

- Select solutions that best overcome your constraints.

- Select solutions that have the greatest amount of support amongst those who will be impacted by the resulting change.

and

- Select the solution which the problem-solver truly believes is the right solution and to which he or she can fully commit so that the solution is effectively implemented.

If the problem-solver is an individual, then he or she will ideally feel that the selection can be made of his or her own volition. If the problem-solver is a couple or group, then each participant should ideally feel respected and utilized in the decision process. Each participant should ideally feel fully understood and that his or her best contributions influenced the decision.

Agree On The Decision-Making Process

Prior to making a selection, first decide on the decision-making method most appropriate for the given situation. The decision process might be obvious if the problem-solver is only one person. He or she would simply decide. However, even an individual could decide whether to:

- Sleep on the information and let his or her subconscious decide and show that decision in a dream or sudden insight.

- Act now on his or her own, and just decide.

- Seek advice from a confidant.

- Canvas several others for their preferences.

- Decide, then invite others to challenge the decision and change his or her mind if feedback is critical.

or

- Select three desired options then give the final choice to someone who would be impacted the most by the decision.

Even as an individual, the problem-solver should clarify in his or her own mind how he or she is going to make the decision so the decision actually gets made.

If the problem-solver is a couple or group, talk about and decide whether or not this particular decision will be made by:

- one person,
- a sub-group,
- majority rule,
- expression of preferences by all involved then decision by the one person with the most authority,
- polling then discussion then majority vote, or
- consensus.

This selection of a specific decision method will separate out the discussion of how to decide from what to decide. During the selection step, conflict can emerge. Often such conflicts are about how to decide but surface when deciding what solution is to be chosen. Solution ideas get murdered when the fight is about how we should decide.

To prevent this, first decide how the decision will be made. The overall process will be more effective and much easier for the participants to understand. Once a decision method has been chosen, then make the decision by that method, and only that method. Don't agree that the majority decides then wind up with members of the minority fighting for a change of decision.

Choosing the decision method in advance should prevent the all too typical occurrence of making decisions by default. Default decisions occur when a group, couple or individual becomes so conflicted over the act of deciding that no overt decision is made. Instead, something else occurs.

Either no action is taken and that becomes the decision, or the problem-solver falls into a compromise situation and picks something that is acceptable – seldom the optimum solution. Instead, by specifying at the beginning of this step how the decision will be made, it will be much easier to proceed with the actual selection of the solutions.

> This might have been determined earlier in the problem-solving process if one of the constraints stipulated that a particular person or group would make the final decision. If so, that constraint would be honored at this step.

Techniques For Improving Selection

There are several techniques and processes that can be used at this step to achieve such goals.

THE SOLUTION PACKAGE

Think in terms of making choices that include more than one solution possibility. One definition of the word *selection* is to "sort out". This step is best approached as one of sorting out the best ideas from the broad list of possible solutions and developing a solution package.

This package can include ideas that complement each other, extend each other, or cover different targets. This package may contain ideas to be implemented all at once, or ideas to be initiated in sequence according to a previously specified order, or the package might contain back-up or contingency ideas to be implemented should the first selected idea fail.

> The Swiss Army knife can serve as a metaphor for this idea. The knife is a pocket knife but it is so much more because it is combined with many other "blades" that also fold up into the handle - cork screw, nail file, screw driver, tweezers, bottle opened, wire stripper, and reamer.

This may be a common-sense technique but it is not one that is used very often. Typically, the problem-solver sets out looking for one solution, finds something that seems to be okay, adopts it, and then either follows through and implements it, or not.

In too typical situations, if the problem-solver is a couple or group, ideas are evaluated as soon as they are stated, criticized beyond survival until one somewhat satisfactory solution emerges as a compromise and that idea is selected as the decision. Because the process was unpleasant and no one is particularly committed to the solution, the idea is seldom implemented or, if applied, only implemented poorly and there is a return to the status quo.

To be a more effective problem-solver, use techniques for generating many ideas, clarifying and elaborating them all, evaluating both the positives and negatives of each idea, and then select the best solution, or if you can, select a pool of solution options that will really work and produce phenomenal results. You have to be able to afford the group of solutions for this to work but your chances of achieving the optimal results are greater.

THE IMPLEMENTER'S DECISION

Probably the most important requirement is to include those who will be called upon to implement the solution(s). Those who implement are usually the ones that best know the field of action in which the solution will be applied and know what they will encounter.

If they are not included, or if they anticipate difficulties implementing a given idea that the problem-solvers have not anticipated, they are not likely to be fully committed to someone else's less-than-adequate idea. As a general rule, include the implementers in the problem-solving process and as much as possible, let the implementer's decide.

This is easy if the problem-solver is only one person and will be the responsible individual that implements the solution(s) including covering all expenses on his or her own. However, if the problem-solver is a couple or group and many people will implement and/or pay for the solution, then all of them are considered implementers and should join in decision-making.

In many cases, it's wise to include anyone who will be impacted by the chosen solution. For example, customers might be impacted by a decision made about products or services. Find ways to include your customers, or at least, include true representatives. You could ask focus groups to select the few solutions that have the most appeal to them from a pool of solution possibilities so you have an idea how the end users will react to the possible decisions you could make.

RE-DECIDE

Norman Maier demonstrated in his research that problem-solving effectiveness increases when a problem-solver solves the same problem twice. It is a useful technique to force oneself to decide, take a break, then return to re-decide by picking new selections with the rule that the first decision cannot be repeated.

Once this second selection has taken place, you now have two solution possibilities to implement, to choose between, or to use in sequence. Somehow this second re-examination of the available information introduces a new perspective and the second choice can, at times, be superior.

REVERSE PERSUASION

If persuasion behavior surfaces in the selection process, it is useful to disrupt and re-direct it. Arguing and loud repetitive statements in favor of a given idea are evidence of persuasion behavior. Such behavior is usually met by a polarized response, matching or exceeding the intensity of the persuasion attempts. Two people wind up fighting over whose idea is best

This behavior interferes with an effective review of all available information and uses up valuable time. This can also happen inside the mind of an individual problem-solver. It is not useful behavior and counter-productive when the goal is finding an optimum or exceptional solution. It's also a typical sign that the effective techniques for earlier steps in the problem-solving process were not used.

In other words, if one participant is arguing strongly for one of the ideas, or if the individual problem-solver is of two or more arguing minds, it is best to interrupt such behavior and channel the same energy to effective and functional interaction. One way to do this is to re-direct the persuasion behavior. Anyone who engages in argumentative behavior should be labeled as the "persuader" whose task it is to provide good reasons for EACH idea.

In another application, if the person has been arguing one idea against another, then he or she is to be instructed to switch sides and argue for the other idea. If two people are polarized, each arguing for their own preference, then they are directed to switch sides and argue for the other person's point of view.

The same process can be done mentally when this is happening in the mind of the individual problem-solver. Having two opposing thoughts in one's head, each being spoken by one of the voices in our minds, the individual can have the voices switch sides.

This should be done until each side is effectively able to consider the other party's point of view. An optimum selection using all points of view will result.

LISTEN TO YOUR SUBCONSCIOUS MIND

Sometimes it pays to sleep on all of the information that has been organized in the preceding steps. Let this information percolate subconsciously as you do other things. Allow the final selection to arise from clues presented in dreams, or how your attention wanders, or what you suddenly become more aware of in your surroundings.

Input from the subconscious mind can come in very indirect and round-about ways. We can get very useful decision cues if we recognize this process. Perhaps, this input comes in the form of forgetting, or conversely in remembering a particular piece of information. It may be in the form of a dream in which the problem-solver sees him or her self successfully or unsuccessfully implementing one of the solutions. It may come as an impulse to review information that was previously undervalued.

Regardless of the form, it pays to attend to subconscious input during the selection process because the greatest part of human information processing occurs outside of conscious awareness. This would be severely limiting if we did not have tremendous (unlimited perhaps) subconscious capacity, but we do.

We think we can quantify and objectify the decision process, but often it is a "gut decision" that takes us in the right direction. Doing the full evaluation of each idea makes this possible. All that information is now available to our subconscious processes, and below our awareness we may be making a decision. By deliberately attending to clues from the subconscious process, our effectiveness at the selection step in problem-solving will escalate.

METHODS TO DECIDE BETWEEN

In some selection situations, the problem-solver may find him or her self stuck in the predicament of having to choose between two equally desirable alternatives. The first thing to do is to determine if, in fact, it's necessary to choose between. Perhaps you're free to choose both and not have to exclude one in favor of the other. Sometimes the simple decision is to select both to be implemented together, separately or in sequence.

However, there are times when limited resources require a decision between two equally desirable solutions. There are several strategies that you can use to resolve this dilemma, essentially different methods to determine if you truly do regard the two options as equal.

1. **Let Someone Else Decide**: If you truly believe both ideas are good and you can't choose between them, then explain the full problem definition to someone else and ask them to pick either one according to their preferences. They should not explain their choice but just say, "I pick that one."

   Your task is to pay close attention to your own reaction. Do you immediately let out a groan with a facial expression indicating that you wish he or she had picked the other one? Conversely, do you experience a sense of relief and a feeling of gladness that the choice has been made? Either way, from your reaction, you will know your own true selection.

   If no phenomenal reaction occurs, then you know you would have done fine with either idea, and may as well go ahead with the selection the other person has made. However, if this person is someone who might feel anxious about the responsibility of having made your choice for you, worrying that something could go wrong, thank him or her for helping you to test your own preference, then make your own choice.

2. **Flip A Coin**: This decision strategy should only be used when you have what appear to be two equal quality solutions. Like the previous exercise, this method is a way of testing whether or not you truly regard both ideas as equal. Designate one idea as heads and the other as tails. Flip the coin very high, letting it

fall to the floor. This is to give yourself enough time to notice your reaction immediately upon launching the coin.

In most cases, you will notice that you will be wishing for one of heads or tails to come up. This would indicate your true preference. You could probably make your selection before the coin even hits the ground. In some cases, you might hold out to see what fate says in the matter.

Upon checking the outcome, notice how you feel about the result. If your reaction is a groan, you know that you really wanted the other solution. Relief suggests that the coin merely agreed with you. If unaffected, you need only rely on the forces of fate directing you to one of two good solutions.

3. **Pick One**: Just simply pick one solution, state it out loud, then do absolutely nothing related to the problem for at least one hour. If you have the luxury of time, wait overnight before confirming or changing your mind. In this interval, completely ignore or distract yourself from thinking about whether you made the right choice. Simply say, "I've decided. It's now done and over with."

Repeat this to yourself particularly if any doubts seem to creep into your thinking. Notice whether you experience a growing confidence in your decision or an increasing tension and anxiousness as your doubt escalates. If the insistence that a decision has been made is met by a matching or escalating anxiousness, then you have, in fact, decided but not as you have originally stated.

These feelings are suggestions that the other parts of you are saying, "Whoa. I don't like this." The indication seems to be that the other idea is the real preference.

This is true within the mind of an individual or within a couple or group. If any part of the couple or group has tension in response to the comment, "The decision has been made.", stop and clarify the feelings and look for reasons to suspect the correctness of the decision. Trust the wisdom of the dissenter's subconscious.

PRIORITIZE IN GROUP

In any group situation where there isn't sufficient time available to arrive at consensus, or where the lower significance of the problem does not warrant the need for consensus, or where there is considerable pressure to resolve the decision by majority rule, then use this technique to get a sense of priorities. Prioritizing can also be useful as a polling procedure to find out how much agreement or disagreement is present before any discussion.

By now, all group members should understand each of the items so that they know the options from which they will make their choice. To prioritize, post a list of all solution options so that group members can readily see them all and be able to write on the list (flip chart, blackboard, white board). An alternative in the electronic world is to have all of the items in a spreadsheet then send the spreadsheet to all members to place their priority rankings in the spreadsheet privately, return the completed sheet and have someone then build a master sheet with all rankings shown. This final sheet could be projected to a wall or large screen.

There are many prioritizing techniques ranging from ranking the items in order of preference to picking the three that each group member favors most. One method uses a forced choice approach where members have to sort through their own levels of commitment to ideas and show the group what they believe should be given the most consideration. Each person is told they have to show their commitment by allocating resources to the ideas they think are most viable.

Give each person some form of tokens, each token type having a different value. These could be poker chips of different colors, coins of different values, or symbols to be written on the available media. For example a red poker chip, quarter, or circle could be worth twenty-five (25) points; a blue poker chip, dime, or square could be worth ten (10) points; and a black poker chip, nickel or triangle could be worth five (5) points. Give each person one red chip, quarter or circle; two blue chips, dimes or squares; and three black chips, nickels or triangles to spend on the ideas they think have the most viability as solutions.

Direct the members to place their points against the items they select (chips or coins thrown in cans designated for each idea, or symbols or the actual amounts written on the media). The members can't break up the 25 points or 10 points or 5 points into smaller units which forces them to pick which idea is their highest preference and so on. However, the members can chose to invest all of their resources on one idea if they think a particular solution is the most optimum solution.

In other words, some members may spend all sixty points on just one idea while other members might chose to spread their points out over as many as six different ideas. Their strongest preference would get the 25 points, their next two preferences could get 10 points each, and their three lowest preferences would get 5 points each.

Tally the points assigned to each idea then prepare a short list with the ideas listed in diminishing order of points assigned. Allow the members to share their reaction to the ranking of these ideas. They may express surprise, satisfaction with the results, or frustration.

Let these reactions emerge and allow people who are not satisfied with the results to explain why. Work to clarify their reasons because this may be a valuable resource to the group. In too many cases, the minority opinion holds the key to finding the optimum solution and the group needs to be careful that it doesn't just drive that opportunity away by majority force.

In some cases, all members might have favored one solution option, which could then lead to a quick consensus decision. On the other hand, the preferences may be divided or spread out over many items, which then creates the need for significant dialogue. Make sure that all members work to fully understand the preferences and reasons for the preferences of all group members before any decision is taken.

Look for real opportunities to select more than one solution. One myth of problem-solving is that there is one best solution to any problem. In fact, many complementary solution options could be implemented achieving much superior results. Once there is a group feeling that full understanding has been achieved, the group could vote on the options, prioritize once again, or act on a consensus that emerged from the understanding.

This approach can also be used even if the problem-solver is an individual. The problem-solver can start narrowing down his or her preferences by "spending" these imaginary resources on a selection of ideas. Once this step has been completed, the problem-solver would only have to look at the much shorter list (no more than six solution possibilities) and then think through which idea or ideas will be chosen as the preferred solution.

The problem-solver could show this shorter list to a neutral party and seek the other person's comments on the problem-solver's thinking. The problem-solver could step away from the shorter list and focus on other things, letting his subconscious reflect on the choices, then revisit the list later and make a final decision. Or, the problem-solver could just pick the top idea, or two or three ideas, as the solution(s) to be implemented.

RECYCLE

If the selection process is proving to be very difficult, it is likely because the preceding steps in the problem-solving process were done less effectively than they could have been. This difficulty will arise if the problem-solver must decide between a limited batch of low quality solution ideas. In such cases, the inability to decide should be regarded as a signal to return to the initial steps and generate the information that was not produced originally.

In truly creative problem-solving, the best ideas tend to emerge thereby producing an "ah ha" phenomenon – "This idea is so obviously the best idea, we have to wonder why we hadn't thought of doing this before now". If the problem-solver hasn't arrived at such a conclusion at the selection step, go back and work through the steps again, as if for the first time.

Such an inability to decide suggests the importance of re-beginning the problem-solving efforts. Recycle back to the first step and feel the need. Work for a comprehensive problem definition. Get new insights as you define the S.P.I.C.E[3]. Expand the time available for brainstorming and encourage weirder and more absurd ideas. Go for more ideas. Then clarify and expand each idea as fully as possible. Don't settle for simply ignoring an idea because it seems too absurd.

Develop it into a workable solution. Do this for more ideas than were considered the first time, then try the selection step again.

Choose The Optimum Solution(s)

Select the idea or a set of ideas that has the greatest potential of achieving the full set of E^3 benefits within your deadline, at a cost that you can afford, while overcoming your real constraints. Upon making that selection, the problem-solver should feel some excitement about getting this new solution into action. The solution must satisfy the problem-solver's eagerness to get the new benefits as soon as possible.

If that enthusiasm is missing, it's likely that an optimum solution has not been selected. It is not enough to decide to do something that only feels adequate or acceptable. Most certainly, if there is more than one problem-solver, the decision should not be a compromise decision. The solution or solutions should excite everyone because the solution will deliver the desired benefits and results, overcome any constraints, and be implemented within the deadline.

If you don't have what you believe is the best solution, then back up and go through the process again; or back-up to the "Generate Solution Possibilities" Step and brainstorm additional ideas; or back up to the "Elaboration" step and work harder on clarifying and expanding the creative ideas into workable solutions; or back-up and re-evaluate any ideas that might have been prematurely rejected. The decision should include solution possibilities where you have both agreement and enthusiasm.

Tough Choices: Some people say there are problems that have no optimal solution or only optimal solutions that the problem-solver can't afford to implement - that the best that can be hoped for is to choose the least damaging of several tough options.

I would argue that no situation is so dire that a better solution can't be identified when approaching the problem with creative thinking, applied in this FIDGET/RELAX approach. Doing this work should result in a better solution that can be applied using the problem-solver's existing resources and within the existing real constraints.

When To Move To The Next Step

The problem-solver is ready to proceed to the next step of action-planning once:

1. A decision has been made to implement a given solution or a set of solutions.

2. The people who must be committed to the solution for it to be effectively carried out have been involved in the selection of the solution or solutions; or they have been informed about the decision and are in full support.

3. The people who will do the implementation are present and able to participate in the next step.

4. The selected solution is fully understood by all those who will be expected to champion and implement it.

You are ready to move to the next step when a clear decision has been made, and the problem-solver feels some enthusiasm about getting the solution put into place.

Transition To The Next Step

If the problem-solver is an individual, review what you have decided, then clarify in your own mind that it is now time to develop your plan for getting the solution implemented.

"Okay, I've chosen the best solution, and now I need to figure out just exactly how I'm going to implement it."

If the problem-solver is more than one person, then one participant needs to proceed by summarizing once more what has been decided. Stipulate that it is now time to specify who will do what, when, how, where, and with what resources.

"This is great. We have a decision that everyone fully supports and a strong expectation that we will get the results we want. It is my understanding that we have decided to … However, to make sure this happens, we need to make a plan for how we will implement this solution. We aren't done yet."

Step Ten:
Action Planning

The problem has not yet been solved. Your solution(s) must first be put into action. However, before that happens, you should plan out how each solution is to be implemented. Clearly specify who will do what, when, where, how, with what resources, and why. Without this clarity, the solution will likely not be properly executed, and hence fail. By developing a thorough action plan, you prevent failure and increase the chances of successful resolution of your problem.

Insight Potential When "Action Planning" – *The problem-solver may discover the details that make a difference between the solution working and not working. By developing the action plan, fundamental weaknesses of the solution might be revealed, thereby preventing implementation of a solution that will only fail. In addition, if there is more than one person involved, this step may reveal slight differences in understanding about what the solution really is and how it is to be implemented. This will allow resolution of any misunderstandings before putting the solution into action.*

Once the problem-solver has arrived at a clear statement of the solution or solutions that are to be implemented, he or she must clarify how this solution will be put into action. It must be clearly specified who will do what, when, where, how, using what resources, and why. By reinforcing the why of each action that is to be taken, the implementer doesn't lose sight of what he or she is working to achieve.

Too many problem-solvers will work to the point of deciding on a solution to their problem, then stop, thinking the problem has been solved. It has not. A solution or solution set has been identified but the problem has not been solved until the solution has been properly and completely put into action. It is all too common for a problem-solver to arrive at a solution, sit back then wonder why nothing has changed. Many work groups discuss a problem, end their meeting, wait for the solution to work, then wonder why nothing is changing.

Many people think group problem-solving is a waste of time because nothing changes. Well, that may be caused by poor problem-solving behavior in earlier steps, but it is more likely the result of failure to create an action plan so everyone knows their role in solution implementation.

Goal Of Action Planning

This step precedes the actual implementation of a solution. The primary objective at this step is to get ready. There are several goals for this step:

- Clearly build an action plan in which the full sequence of action steps are defined and ordered in the optimum order.

- Make sure that all implementers are aware of their role so everyone knows what they have to do.

- Uncover and resolve any differences in understanding about just how the solution is to work.

and

- Build confidence that the solution can be effectively implemented and will work.

152

The Elements Of An Action Plan

There are many details that affect the implementation of any solution. This step allows the problem-solver to address each of the details that matter. Action planning requires clarity in ten different dimensions:

Activities	The behaviors and actions that are specifically supposed to happen.
Sequence	The specific order in which the behaviors and actions are to take place.
Trigger	The event or action that triggers the start of the implementation process
Timing	The timeline when each action is specifically supposed to take place.
Signals	The specific signals that indicate "go" to the person responsible for the next action .
Roles	The collection of actions that each person is responsible for completing during the implementation period.
Checks	The persons or person who will check to see that the sequence is being completed in the appropriate progressive order, and make sure that the sequence is repaired if broken.
Location	The specific location where each action is supposed to take place.
Resources	The resources that are to be available at each location to be used for each action.
Rewards	The benefits each person in the action sequence realizes when he or she has completed each of his or her parts of the plan.

Work to make sure that your plan has specific details for each of these ten dimensions. Be as specific and as clear as possible so there is little room for misunderstanding. Each person should know exactly what is expected of him or her, and when he or she is to act.

Techniques For Action Planning

There are several techniques and processes that are useful to help the problem-solver develop an action plan that will work.

RECORD THE PLAN

Write out the plan of action. By externalizing the plan and making it visible for scrutiny, it's much easier to detect missing aspects of the plan. As well, this written record serves as a stimulant for more complete thinking about all aspects of the plan. Most importantly, this written record serves as a reference point later in the implementation step.

Using a computer, project management software can be used to facilitate this process of both planning and recording the plan. All the elements of effective planning are built into such computer programs to insure that the project is properly planned and managed.

In most situations, there is a delay between selection of a solution and the implementation of that solution. Often the implementation period itself is one of considerable time. By having a written record, the problem-solver can use this visual guide like a road map, referring to it periodically, to remind him or her as to what to do next. This record also serves as a checklist to monitor what has already been accomplished and what is yet to come.

BE SPECIFIC

In order for a plan to work, and to increase the probability that the plan will be carried out, the problem-solver needs to be very specific in his or her plans. Use descriptive terms rather than general terms.

The plan should indicate details of the specific behavior to be used to solve the problem rather than a general conclusion to do better. For example, if a problem-solver is working on a problem to reduce his or her eating, rather than a statement like, "I'll eat less", the specific behaviors would be to "weigh what is to be eaten, determine the caloric value, and only serve that amount that fits within the desired calorie intake".

The plan should clearly specify who will do what, where, when, how, with what resources, and why. People need to know where and how they will do what they are assigned to do, and why they are to do it this way. If people have very clear instructions about their part in the solution implementation, there is no confusion that trips one person up and then causes delays or failure that prevents the next person in the sequence from doing his or her part.

The plan should also be very specific about the timing of the specific behaviors. Specify exactly when each behavior should happen. Identify the signals or cues that should be present to indicate the behavior is now appropriate.

General plans don't work for several reasons. When the action plan is not specific, the problem-solver will only have a vague expectation for what is to happen. He or she will not have a real understanding of what should be done differently and will be inclined to stick with status quo behaviors.

If the terminology is general, it is hard to know exactly what the proper actions are in the new situation with a new solution. Err on the side of being extra specific so that it is clear what is to happen. Compare these two action statements:

General	Specific
"Communicate better."	"Before you express your own opinion, paraphrase what the last person said until three things happen - the other person says you understand, you know you understand, and the other person says he or she understands him or herself better."

If no specific timing assignments are made, then it is very hard to have predictability, regularity and consistency in the application of the new behavior that is specified in the plan. A solution that isn't implemented in a clear and sequential fashion isn't likely to succeed.

The plan needs to make sure each participant does their part when their part is next called for, so the sequence stays intact.

For example:

Example 1

GENERAL
I'll be more honest with Brian in the future.

SPECIFIC
Next time that I see Brian, I will suggest that we talk about how we affect each other. If he agrees, I will tell him that I am having difficulty working with him when he doesn't speak directly to me or even look at me. I will ask him to look me in the eye when he speaks with me. Then I will ask him to paraphrase me to be sure he understands my feedback and request.

If he doesn't understand, I will find another way to express what I need, then ask him to paraphrase again. If he understands, I will tell him that I'm satisfied that he does understand and I will ask him if he is okay with my request. I will paraphrase to make sure I understand his reaction fully and that he knows I understand.

If he agrees to what I'm asking, I will thank him for listening and for his commitment to try this new way of communicating. I will ask him if there is anything I need to change that would make his communicating with me easier for him.

If he doesn't agree to talk with me, or if he doesn't agree to honor my request for eye contact when he talks with me, I will suggest that we meet with his boss to discuss my concerns and explore a mutually satisfactory solution.

Example 2

GENERAL
Now that I have finished high school, it would probably be best to find my own home and experience living on my own.

SPECIFIC

I'm going to leave here, purchase a paper, look at the apartment rental section, immediately telephone five or six places and find out how much money is involved in moving out on my own. If accommodation is offered for less than $1,200 per month, I will arrange to see what is offered. If I can find something that will work for my needs and if I can obtain a place for the beginning of the month, I'll take it and tell my family by Saturday.

Implementation in these two examples is considerably more likely when the action plan is specific than it is in the corresponding general statements.

One failure is all that it takes to cause participants to resort back to status quo behaviors. The more specific the plan is regarding the ten dimensions, the better the chance of successful implementation. Essentially, your plan can't be too detailed. Your problem-solving performance is directly related to an effective execution of a detailed plan of action.

FLOW-CHARTING

Flow-charting forces a problem-solver to deliberately consider all ten elements of an action plan and visually organize all the actions in their order. Diagram the flow of activities and events that are to occur between commencement and completion of the implementation. This can be done manually or by using specific project management software that generates such charts.

A flow chart identifies which activities can occur simultaneously and which must occur sequentially. Flow charting forces the action planner to be specific and deliberate in describing the trigger that should initiate implementation; the activities that are to occur; the sequence in which these activities are to occur so that each next activity has what it needs to be implemented; and the signals that show an activity has been completed and the next action should be initiated. In addition, key checkpoints are specified so that the problem-solver is observing and assessing progress toward the E^3 desired outcomes.

There are many different formats for diagramming a flow chart. One useful format is to start at the initial trigger point that indicates the implementation should begin. A large arrow would then point to those activities that can happen immediately without having to be preceded by anything other than the trigger to start. Each of these activities would be described inside its own circle on the flow chart. A line would then point from the activity to a square, which would then contain a description of the output of that activity as the signal that the activity has been completed.

Some activities must be completed at the same time to produce the various outputs that are needed in an activity that follows. In that way, these activities are related. Bracket lines can show that relationship.

Flow Chart Example

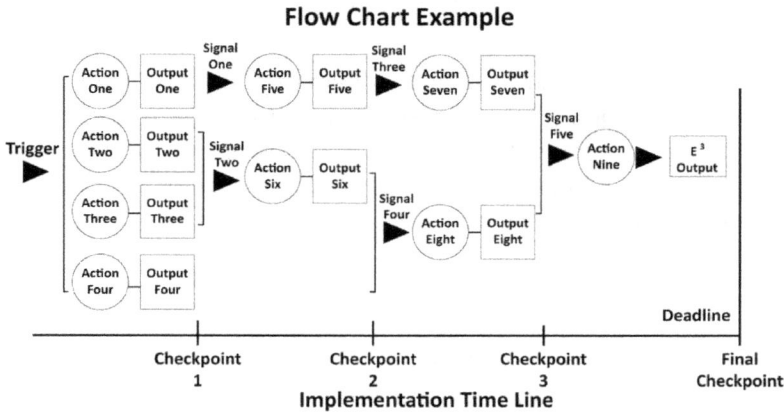

This process continues until all activities and their outcomes have been mapped. The final outcome in the flow chart should be the E^3 outcomes that were specified in the S.P.I.C.E^3 problem definition. The end result should reflect the minimal expectations, the most desired outcomes and the eagerness that the problem-solver has to achieve these desired results (deadline).

Once the chart has been diagrammed, it's a simple task to make specific role assignments by ascribing individuals' names to each activity on the chart. This becomes a highly visible reminder for each participant as to what he or she should do when. In the case of a single problem-solver, this may encourage him or her to think about soliciting help from others and adding their names to the chart.

Next, the locations for each activity can be recorded on the flow chart indicating where the action is to take place. This causes recognition of how the outputs must be moved from one location to another to be available for the next-in-order activity. This might hi-light the need for other activities associated with the relocation of outputs and these can be added to the chart.

The necessary resources needed for each activity can also be entered so each individual knows the tools and other materials they will need to have in order to complete their portion of the implementation. It gives them a clear indication what they need so they can acquire more when running low.

The rewards the individuals can expect for completing their activities successfully and on time can be added to show even more specificity. This answers the question, "what's in it for me" and adds to each individual's motivation to do his or her part correctly.

Once all of this information has been organized in this fashion, each participant has a complete picture of the action plan. There are software programs available to produce such flow charts when the implementation plan is very complex, and technology available to produce large format prints of such charts so they can be posted in work locations for easy reference. Use the technology available to you to make the implementation plan as visual as possible.

SET A CLEAR IMPLEMENTATION PERIOD

It's very important to specify the implementation period. By setting a time when the implementation is to start and a time by which the implementation period is to be complete, the problem-solver can work toward this deadline. This deadline for completion gives urgency to the successful completion of all of the tasks.

In some cases, a solution will result in failure if not completed on time. By being clear about the implementation period, the problem-solver knows that this is a critical component of success and will work more urgently toward complete implementation. Each participant should know and understand the importance of both the start and end dates.

ROLE ASSIGNMENT VARIATIONS

In cases where a group will implement the solution, each member will be assigned different responsibilities. There are several options available when making individual role assignments so that each participant has a specific part to play in the implementation process. The method chosen should be a function of the significance of the problem. Where the potential gains are very high then the assignment of responsibilities should be much more deliberate and matched to expertise. If the consequences of failure are lower, then the assignment of responsibilities can be more casual.

Volunteering

One obvious method is to clearly define all of the activities that need to be done and then allow individuals to volunteer to carry out those activities that they personally have some incentive to implement. This method matches activities by commitment thereby increasing the likelihood that the solution will be fully implemented.

It is possible that some necessary activities will be seen as undesirable and not selected in this voluntary process. In such a case, extra incentives must be provided to cause someone to take on that commitment. The person must feel that the rewards match the task.

Training

In this approach, participants are assigned activities they are not used to performing with the expectation that they will acquire new skills in doing so, and thereby master the new activity. This method has particular utility in those problem situations in which the risk of a poor quality implementation is not that great. The costs of potential failure should be seen as less than the potential benefits of the training outcome.

This method is also useful when the activities have been so clearly defined and described that each learner can be expected to carry them out and experience the satisfaction of successful contribution to the whole. There are times in problem-solving where the long run perspective has primacy and this method of assignment would be the best one to use.

Matching To Expertise

In this approach, people are assigned tasks and activities based on expertise. Those persons most skilled in performing specific tasks would be assigned to those activities within the action plan. This method of assignment is most appropriate when the activities are complex, the costs of error are too expensive, and the potential gain from successful implementation is very high. Matching assignments to expertise is more likely to ensure that the action plan is implemented effectively.

Mixed Methods Of Assignment

Some tasks and activities might be very complex. These could be assigned based on expertise. Some tasks might be good training opportunities for some participants to build their proficiencies and could be assigned on that basis. Other tasks might best be assigned based on individual desire to do them. The mixed method approach requires deep and open discussion by the participants to make sure that the assignments are best arranged and to make sure that all participants have confidence that implementation will work flawlessly.

THE BIG TEN CHECKLIST

After the problem-solver thinks he or she has completed a full action plan, it is helpful to read or review the plan to ensure that the plan clearly indicates all ten important dimensions. Read the plan looking for detail and find the aspects of the plan that specify:

- the trigger,
- all activities,
- the sequence of activities,
- the timing expected for completion of each of the activities and the deadline for full implementation,
- the signals that should initiate each activity,
- the roles of each participant which include each person's activities,
- the location of each step in implementation,
- the check points at which progress will be measured and the elements to be assessed for each activity to ensure compliance with the plan,
- the resources to be used during each activity, and

- the rewards for completion of each activity.

Review the plan and place a check mark on the list as you determine that each element has been covered. This makes sure that all the important dimensions to action planning are covered before implementation is initiated. If something is missing, implementation will break down, leading the participants to see the solution as a failure and resort back to the status quo.

THE 7W QUESTIONS

Up until now, the importance of the ten dimensions has been emphasized. However some problems only require very simple action plans because the solutions are brief one or two act events. In such cases, it's enough for the problem-solver to make a quick summary statement which answers the seven basic questions – "Who is going to do what, where, when, how, with what resources, and why?" Even though the answers to a given problem situation may appear obvious, it is extremely useful to verbalize and record them.

PERSONAL COMMITMENT LIST

The problem-solver may be an individual so all tasks and activities will be completed by him or her. A flow chart could still be completed but it might be enough to make a personal commitment list that contains all the things the problem-solver will do in the order in which he or she will do them. The last item in the list should summarize the E^3 outcome that the problem-solver has determined he or she wants to achieve by solving the problem.

By writing out this series of tasks as personal commitment statements, the problem-solver has a checklist to hold him or herself responsible for completing the tasks as and when they should be completed:

- I will…
- Then I will...
- Then I will…
- Because I want…

This is a variation of the "To Do" list. By writing each task as a commitment statement, the problem-solver is making a clear declaration that he or she will follow-through with the complete implementation. Such commitments can be very useful because the draw to return to the status quo is very strong. By closing with a clear statement of the desired benefits to be achieved by implementing the solution, the problem-solver reminds him or herself why these tasks must be done successfully.

This can also be used when the problem-solver is more than one person. If each person writes out their own commitment list and shares it with the others, then there is an increased likelihood that each person will fulfill his or her part.

When To Move To The Next Step

You will know you are ready to proceed to the next step where the solution is actually implemented when you have:

- specified clearly who is going to do what, where, when, how, with what resources, and why,

- specified what is to be the trigger that indicates implementation can begin,

- specified the order in which everything is to take place,

- prescribed the checkpoints by which you will be able to recognize whether or not the action plan is operating as it should, and

- prepared a written record of the plan for easy visual reference.

When you have satisfied the above criteria, you're ready for implementation.

Transition To The Next Step

At the appropriate time, the solution will be put into action. The time to begin should have been specified clearly in the action plan and the person who is responsible for saying "Go" should have been identified. That person would declare:

"According to our plan, it's time to begin the implementation of our solution. You know what you have to do and when. Begin the first step."

Step Eleven: eXecute

To solve the problem, the plan must be put into action and the solution implemented. In the process of executing the solution, there are still some things a problem-solver can do to minimize the costs of any failure and increase the chance of success.

Insight Potential When "eXecuting" – *The problem-solver may discover that the solution works as intended, or alternatively that the solution fails to generate the desired results within the deadline, or the results might far exceed expectations; or the problem-solver might discover that certain details were not satisfactorily addressed in the action plan and changes need to be made so the solution can be implemented properly; or the problem-solver might discover that this solution works but introduces some new problems that have to be resolved.*

You've reached this stage because you felt an itch for something to change, defined the S.P.I.C.E^3 of your situation, brainstormed a large number of solution possibilities, elaborated and clarified those options, evaluated them by looking for the best aspects of each idea before considering weaknesses, made a selection of a solution or a package of solutions, then mapped out a sufficiently comprehensive implementation plan. Now, it's time to get this problem solved.

Goals Of This Step

The most significant goals of this step in the problem-solving process are to:

- Fully implement the plan.

- Prevent failure or reduce the costs of failure to the lowest possible level.

- Increase the chances of success.

- Measure progress along the way to full implementation.

- Make adjustments if the encounter with reality means that the implementation plan is breaking down.

- Achieve the specified $\mathbf{E^3}$ outcomes, thereby closing the problem gap.

- Meet any deadlines for full implementation.

and

- Feel significant satisfaction with the change process and the changes accomplished.

A successful implementation will achieve all of these goals. If so, the problem will be solved thereby creating a new status quo in which the payoffs and benefits exceed what was being achieved in the old one.

Techniques For Effective Implementation

There are various things the problem-solver can do to be more effective at the implementation step. Too many problem-solvers think the solution will somehow materialize and that all will be okay. Care must be taken during implementation to ensure that the solution is truly applied as it was intended to be, and that it is not breaking down during the implementation step.

MONITOR PROGRESS

Track progress with particular consideration for whether or not everything is progressing on time, and whether or not each of the activities produces the necessary outcomes. Look for weaknesses in the action plan that can be corrected before it is too late. Fix any issues so that the ultimate deadline can be met.

By monitoring progress at each of the checkpoints, the problem-solver can determine if the plan is working as intended. Monitoring could show that the implementation plan is working flawlessly and the problem-solver can be reassured that the right plan is in place. If a well-developed action plan is monitored during implementation and is discovered to not be working as intended, the problem-solver must stop, adjust, and make a new plan. Fix the points where the plan is breaking down and monitor for improvement.

However, in some situations, by monitoring progress, it may become evident to the problem-solver that the solution is not solving the problem. In such an instance, the problem-solver must acknowledge the need to choose a new solution alternative. Backed by the surety that the solution was implemented as intended, the problem-solver can let go of that solution when confronted with evidence that it is not working.

Many problem-solvers feel locked into the solution choice even when overtly confronted with evidence that the solution does not solve the problem. Often because of a lack of a clear action plan, or any certainty that the right action plan has been followed, the assumption is made that the solution was not implemented properly. This leads to the craziness of intensified efforts to make the solution work because "it was the one we chose and we have to stick to it."

Setting time limits for each stage of implementation and building in checkpoints reduces the likelihood of this occurring. If a well-developed plan has been followed, and the solution does not achieve the goals, then the time bounded implementer will be able to acknowledge the need to stop, back up and choose a new solution.

166

IMPLEMENTATION BY TRIAL

It's often possible, and wise, to set up safe, low risk, manageable trials of the solutions or solution package. It's not necessary to always risk everything on a full implementation. Full implementation takes on the risk of dramatic change before fully knowing if the solution will actually work and actually achieve the E^3 outcomes.

As well as providing an opportunity for a test of the solution(s), using a trial provides a good opportunity for rehearsal and fine-tuning. Confidence is built up by implementing in sub-scale situations before taking on the full-scale problem.

Too often, problem-solvers come up with what they think is a solution and proceed to implement without much of a plan and without understanding the risks being taken by fully implementing an untried solution. Such efforts typically lead to failure of either the implementation, or the solution, or both, with costly consequences. If a trial were conducted first, any weaknesses in either the implementation plan or the solution would be discovered before the full costs of failure would result.

There are different methods for trial implementation:

Pilot
One common method is to identify an easily defined subset or example of the real problem situation and try the solution out only on that smaller sample. Business enterprises might identify a representative sample of their market and use the new solution only in that smaller sample. If the strategy fails in the pilot, the costs of implementation are not as drastic as they would have been in a full implementation. If the pilot succeeds, everyone has greater confidence the solution will work in the larger context.

Individuals could try the solution out in a safer context. If the solution doesn't work there, then corrective action must be taken before attempting to deal with a riskier context. For example, the solution could be tried out with family before attempting to implement it at work.

By implementing a solution as a trial, it means that the solution will be evaluated before it is imposed totally. This can make the change process more tolerable because we know we can revert back to the old status quo if the new solution doesn't produce the desired E^3 outcomes, or at least outcomes that are better than the old status quo. Plus, when everything works as intended, the benefits of adopting the solution can be shown to exceed the costs of doing so, creating a much more positive expectation that the solution will work as it should.

Role-Play Rehearsal

In some problem situations, particularly those involving interpersonal interaction, it's possible to conduct a trial implementation by role-playing the real life situation using the new solution. This allows the implementers to explore how they would respond to the reactions of others in the role-play.

As well, those who will actually be impacted by the solution could be invited and involved in the role-play. Each person could then share how the solution felt to him or her. Such feedback, like the thermostat controlling the furnace, may trigger minor adjustments to the solution action plan or to the solution itself, or may demonstrate early on that the solution is not going to deliver the desired E^3 outcomes.

Theatre groups have full dress rehearsals the night before the performance of a play is to go active. Launch teams often rehearse a launch before the real thing. Surgeons in training rehearse on cadavers. Race car drivers take newly serviced vehicles out on the track before a real race to make sure everything is working as planned.

Role-playing is a highly recommended technique when the problem situation is an interactional one and there is very little need for expensive resources or props to test the solution out. Find out if the solution will work in a low risk rehearsal.

Mock-Up Simulation

This technique is similar to conducting a role-play rehearsal but it is an extension of that approach in that it requires a replica of the environment in which the solution is to be used, and a mock-up of any equipment that is to be used as part of the solution. A mock-up has more cost to it than a simple rehearsal but might be required when the environment and tools play a key role in the implementation.

Canadian military leaders revolutionized military strategy during the First World War (WWI) when they fully rehearsed a planned battle to recover control of Vimy Ridge in France. They built mock-ups of the battlefield and rehearsed their battle plan. Because all participants knew their role and the whole battlefield strategy, the Canadian forces were victorious despite heavy casualties. The outcome shocked everyone as they took the ridge in one day of battle. It had previously been assumed by other allied military leaders that the best they could achieve was a month's worth of holding action to keep the enemy from advancing.

Smart business has used simulation in new product development. The new product is made first in mock-up form to see if it works. The advent of 3D printers makes this process even less expensive and more effective.

Despite its obvious utility, this implementation technique is often not used when it should be. This is most true in problem situations involving human interactions. Because the problems are regarded as technical issues and not human issues, the problem-solver may fail to acknowledge and recognize the important interface between the people involved and the physical environments and technical processes involved within the solution.

Unfortunately, despite an increasing sophistication on the part of industrial designers, commercial products continue to appear with design flaws or inadequacies that lead to failure in the marketplace. Designers of equipment, buildings, transportation devices, appliances, software, communities, furniture, etc. still continue to develop and proffer new solutions which fail to account for the human-environment-tools interaction.

For example, traffic designers are frequently accused of oversights – failure to build for growth in traffic, not anticipating changed traffic patterns, ignoring environmental factors that cause roads and equipment to fail, underestimating the needs for software proficiency to manage traffic flow, etc. In another example, I was unable to do my on-line banking over a period of two days because my bank fully implemented a software update that provided a messed up customer login screen and completely blocked customer access.

All of these situations would have been prevented if the solution had been put through a trial in advance of full-scale implementation. Mock-up simulation, now easily facilitated by computer, would alleviate such difficulties and lead to ultimate solutions that are known to work before full-scale implementation.

The mock-up requires re-creation of the environment in which the solution is to be used so that the problem-solver has a better opportunity to see, hear, feel the effects of the solution on others, the environment and oneself. This re-creation process involves cost. The cost of such an approach has to be compared to the potential pay-off plus the costs if the solution were to ultimately fail.

The potential pay-off is a function of the importance of the problem and the perceived benefits of both the rehearsal and the ultimate solution plus the accrued advantages achieved via fine-tuning the action plan or the solution. The potential costs of failure include both what could be lost when an inadequate solution is implemented plus the costs of returning the situation to the status quo – the cost of recovery.

As much as possible, the mock-up should duplicate the real situation and emphasize the most difficult aspects, but a complete match to the real situation is seldom achievable. It's possible to do a successful mock-up exercise and still have the full solution fail when applied in the real situation. The solution might work during the mock trial but subsequently fail because an unanticipated variable appears in real life and effectively overwhelms the planned solution.

For example, the American rescue mission for the hostages held in Iran during the early 80's was practiced over and over to test the planned solution. However, dessert weather and the effects of sand on the military equipment were underestimated and the mission failed. Severe dust storms disabled three of the eight helicopters sent on the mission causing the mission to be aborted.

This is always a risk in mock-up simulations. This risk can be countered by emphasizing the worst things that could happen to see how the solution bears up under pressure and by making sure the mock-up is as close to real life situations as possible.

However, there will be times when the problem-solver knows that a solution will break down if certain events are precipitated or randomly occur but will still elect to proceed with a real life implementation of that solution. Because of the absolute need to take some action, and the belief that the solution has the greatest chance of working most effectively, there are times when it may be necessary to gamble that events turnout in favor of the solution.

The mock-up serves to warn of potential breakdowns. At least with a mock-up simulation, the problem-solver has a realistic idea of possible unfavorable developments and will not be caught off guard. Contingency plans can be put into effect anticipating what might go wrong.

MULTIPLE IMPLEMENTATIONS

Sometimes it's useful to implement different solutions at the same time. The problem-solver may want to find out which solution is going to have what effect. This can be determined by marking out special situations where each solution is tried.

For example, the problem may be one of dealing with chronic callers to "Help" or "Distress" lines. All such services have the problem of too frequent, less needy users who block off the telephone lines from other more needy callers who may be in serious distress, only to chat with the volunteer answering the phone. Four solutions might be developed. By trying one solution with the first chronic caller, another with the second and so on, the problem-solver can monitor the results of each solution and determine which is working best. This may lead to simple implementation of all solutions for all

171

calls, only one solution for all calls, or any special combination of the solutions according to the type of call or caller.

Such a technique of applying a given solution in a subsection of the real life problem is another way to generate information about the effects of the implementation before full implementation actually occurs. By applying the solution in a small sub-sector, the costs of failure are reduced, the learning potential is increased, and confidence in the solution grows when it works in the smaller context.

MAKE IT FUN AND PROVIDE REFRESHMENTS

Build in ways to make implementation fun. By providing specific moments of relief either by taking breaks, diverting attention, or through the use of humor, the implementation phase can be elevated to an enjoyable, intrinsically pleasurable event. If the implementers perceive the task as one of onerous labor or tedium, motivation to perform the task and follow the action plan will decrease and performance will decline. If the implementer feels like he or she is having fun, then that enjoyment transfers to higher motivation to do the job well.

Refreshment can be a literal technique whereby the problem-solver structures specific nourishment breaks into the action plan at significant points of implementation, or refreshment can be a figurative technique whereby the problem-solver challenges his or her own creativity to find ways to install fun within the act of carrying out the solution. This does not mean that you should take the implementation step lightly. It means you are encouraged to have fun doing something of importance.

PLAY-BY-PLAY

Behaviorally, this technique involves speaking out loud or presenting public written notices that given activities have taken place and achieved the desired outcomes. This is a reminder that there is a plan in place, the plan is being followed, that everyone has done his or her part to that point, and that there is a reward by acknowledgement of performance.

As a youngster, I played hockey with another fellow who had aspirations to be a radio announcer. As kids tend to do, he enjoyed his own fantasies. In our hockey games, he could be heard to call his own play-by-play as he skated, passed, checked others, and shot the puck. He even did this while sitting on the bench, calling the play-by-play action of those on the ice. His performance as a player, and the play of our team was very noticeably better when he conducted this ongoing play-by-play broadcast. We all had a little more fun when this fellow was having fun doing his play-by-play announcing.

Some problem-solvers may initially find this technique difficult to use because of various embarrassments about being so public. However, this tension interferes with effective implementation anyway so efforts should be made to relieve participants from such inhibitions.

If concerned about image, the problem-solver need only try this by announcing to him or her self and others when major activities and events have taken place. Such out loud comments fit the context and tend not to be perceived as anything more than the enjoyment of doing well and the satisfaction of completing one's own contribution. Progress could be recognized at group meetings, in regular newsletters, or in state of the union e-mails.

When To Move To The Next Step

Yes, there is a next step even after the solution has been fully implemented. You're ready to move to the next step when you have:

- followed the full action plan and implemented the complete solution or solution package,
- implemented the solution before the deadline, or
- the action plan has broken down.

When the above criteria have been met, you're ready to conduct a follow-up assessment of your problem-solving effort.

Transition To The Next Step

There is a natural tendency to evaluate the outcome of any new implementation but such evaluation tends to be shallow in nature. We commonly finish implementation then quickly look at the results and think, "Hurray!" or "Crap!", depending on the outcome, and then act like it's over.

This is not helpful. There is a learning opportunity here that we should take advantage of. This step is deliberately part of effective problem-solving.

If the problem-solver is an individual, he or she now needs to exercise personal discipline and think to him or her self:

> "I need to stop and do a comprehensive evaluation of the results I've achieved, and then, I need to think through the process I used while working on this problem. I want to see if anything better could have been achieved, and how I could have problem-solved more effectively."

If the problem-solver is a couple or group, one of the participants needs to bring the focus around to an effective assessment of both the final results achieved by the solution, and an assessment of the problem-solving process itself. The participant needs to urge everyone to learn from this experience.

> "Okay, now that we've fully implemented our solution, we need to get together and study both the results we achieved, and how well we worked together as a problem-solving group. Did the solution achieve the E^3 goals, exceed them, or fall short? Did we work through the problem-solving sequence as well as we could have? "

The Finish

You've travelled through the FIDGETy first half of the problem-solving process. Hopefully this has been a stage of uncertainty, hunches, random thinking - a creative process generating many solution possibilities. And then you engaged in further creativity by elaborating on each of the ideas. You took a break, then entered into the RELAX half of the process. You used your critical judgement. You evaluated each of the ideas then locked onto the solution or set of solutions that you believed to be optimum. You formed an action plan and executed. Hopefully, you have relaxed into your new status quo and achieved the better results you wanted. It would appear that you're done. However, you still have to Finish this particular problem-solving event.

Step Twelve: Assess Results And Your Process

You want to make sure you achieved the intended results. You also want to learn from this particular experience. This last step involves measurement of the results that you achieved and a hindsight examination of the process you followed to get to that solution. Determine if the desired E^3 outcome has been achieved. Measure the results and quantify what you accomplished. Then, work out why the results turned out as they did. Use hind-sight and review the problem-solving process you followed. Look at how you did each step. If you didn't get the intended results, try to establish where your problem-solving efforts came up short. Determine if anything could have been done more effectively. If you achieved what you intended, or even more than you intended, try to ascertain where you were particularly effective so you can repeat that in future problem-solving situations.

Insight Potential When "Assessing" – *In examining the results achieved by your solution, you may discover that you achieved what you intended, fell short, or exceeded your hoped for results. You may also realize that the newly created status quo has problems of its own, thereby requiring new problem-solving activity. In turn, in looking at how you worked on the problem, you might discover weaknesses in what you did and be able to identify what to concentrate on doing better when working on your next problem. Alternatively, you might recognize that new strengths in your problem-solving behavior appeared and led you to a better than anticipated outcome.*

After the solution has been put into action, the problem-solver needs to determine if the solution accomplished what was intended. Did the solution result in the desired E^3 outcomes? Did it meet minimum expectations? Did it provide the highly desirable benefits the problem-solver hoped to achieve? Did the solution satisfy the problem-solver's eagerness to bring about a change to achieve a better order of being? Was the deadline met? The problem definition showed the problem gap – the difference between where the problem-solver was and where he or she wanted to be. It's important to ascertain if this gap was closed.

In addition, completing the problem-solving process is an important opportunity to learn more about effective problem-solving. The problem-solver also needs to determine if the methods used to problem solve worked effectively in this instance. Were various techniques used effectively? Did information emerge after problem-solving that should have been considered during? Did the problem-solver completely follow the steps in their logical order, or did he or she jump around in the steps confusing him or her self or any others engaged in joint problem-solving?

Goals Of The Assessment Step

After problem-solving, assess what you've done and establish whether or not you:

- arrived at the best possible solution(s),

- used a problem-solving process that most effectively processed information and gave you the best chance to find the optimum solution(s),

- utilized all of the capabilities of the problem-solver(s) and achieved personal satisfaction during the problem-solving event,

- enjoyed yourself (yourselves) during the problem-solving activity, and

- enriched yourself (yourselves) by effectively growing and developing through the solutions you found.

This follow-up assessment addresses the quality of the solution and the quality of the process. The solution has to work and the problem-solver has to feel okay about how the solution was arrived at and implemented.

Ongoing Assessment

It's important to note that process assessment doesn't have to wait until the problem-solving is over. The problem-solving process can be evaluated during the act of problem-solving, and should be. Assess how well you're doing as you're doing it. Any weaknesses can be identified and corrective action can be instituted so that the process improves and the final outcome is optimum.

Pay attention to the quality of the information that you gather together, your process of gathering and organizing the information, and the degree of enjoyment and satisfaction that you have as the work is being done. If the problem-solver is a couple or group, periodically check to see that all participants are satisfied with the process and progress. There are various ways to do this while problem-solving.

RITUALISTIC CHECKS

Each time that a particular problem-solving step is completed, ask yourself about the quality of the work you did on that step. If an individual, ask yourself, "Did I uncover all of the important information for this part of the problem-solving process?" If a couple or group, ask yourselves, "Did we work well together and bring out all of the important information that was needed at this stage? Did we work cooperatively or were we competing with each other to get our preferred solution selected by the group?" Develop a useful set of assessment questions to use when doing these ritualistic checks.

ONGOING SATISFACTION INDEX

You could periodically stop and give yourself a satisfaction rating. Use a 1 to 10 scale where 10 means highly satisfied. Rate how satisfied you are with your performance so far. You could record a rating of the quality of your results at the end of each step and another rating for your quality of process.

For problem-solving over several days, at the end of each day, record a satisfaction rating in a daily diary. These ratings can be referred to later in your follow-up assessment. If the problem-solving process leads to failure, you can look back to see where it may have broken down. The act of recording such satisfaction ratings as you proceed can also lead to correction in mid-process and increase the chances of arriving at an optimum solution.

TAKE THE PROBLEM-SOLVER'S TEMPERATURE

In couple or group problem-solving situations, periodically stop to find out how everyone is feeling about working together. This allows each participant to indicate whether or not he or she likes what is happening as the couple or group proceeds and whether or not he or she feels confident about how well the group is doing. Ask, "Is there anything we could be doing better?"

By stopping for a few moments to assess how everything is proceeding, any necessary corrective action can be taken early in the process. The participants may need to stop and clarify which process they are using. Or the participants may need to stop and check to see if everyone is satisfied that the group is gathering and considering all of the important information. Does anyone feel his or her input is being ignored or that important information was prematurely discarded?

By checking how each group member feels about the problem-solving activity, it may be affirmed that everything is okay and then the group can proceed with confidence. If everything is going well, the group can feel excitement and anticipation about arriving at an optimum solution. If things aren't going well, corrective action can adjust the process and bring the group back to that feeling of excitement and anticipation.

* * *

Whether or not you conduct your follow-up assessment at the end of each problem-solving step or at the end of having implemented the full solution, you need to do follow-up assessment. Earlier is better because you can make corrections to the process you are using. However, you need to do a follow-up assessment for sure. Minimally, you need to evaluate after the solution has been implemented to measure the results. A further assessment of the process, looking at it in hindsight, would also be of value even if you assessed after each step.

Techniques For Assessment

There are various techniques that can be used to improve your performance at this stage in the problem-solving process.

INVITE EVALUATIVE FEEDBACK

Someone else can often provide the most effective follow-up assessment. A very useful technique is to show others what you've done and how you've done it, and then invite their constructive comments. The outsider's perspective may be useful because of its freshness.

Even when the outsider is a naïve observer, his or her perceptual difference may point out something of which you were not aware. In addition, notice how you feel about what you're telling this person. Any embarrassment, tension, or reservations that you have about what you reveal to this other person can point to your own areas of discomfort or the doubts you have about either the process you used or the quality of your solution.

Getting feedback from others expands your own ability to assess the outcome and the process you used. You have both what they tell you and your own impressions, so use the information that works best for you.

FISHBOWL YOUR PROBLEM-SOLVING PROCESS

Every now and then, if you have enough people available to do this, it is a beneficial exercise to problem-solve out loud while others observe. This performance, like the fish in a goldfish bowl, makes for a personal consciousness about what you are doing. Being watched by others reinforces self-monitoring. We tend to be more self-conscious and aware of what we're doing when we know others are watching.

However, this exercise also provides useful feedback about your performance from the watchers. At the end of your problem-solving process, ask them what they noticed. They can freely comment about both the quality of your result and the quality of your process. By allowing others to observe your behavior, you can improve your performance.

BEHAVIORAL ANALYSIS VIA TAPE RECORDING

If problem-solving as a couple or group, tape record the discussion throughout the entire problem-solving process, then replay the tape with a structured analysis tool. Doing this, allows you to identify what happened during your discussion as you worked together.

We call this exercise "mapping your problem-solving process". The Chart for Mapping Your Problem-Solving Process (see Appendix 4) is a useful tool for doing this exercise. Also see Appendix 4 for instructions. Appendix 5 contains samples of statement types that fit within each of the steps and will help you figure out where to place your checkmarks for each statement in your discussion.

This process can be used to determine if you followed an organized and sequential movement through the steps or bounced around, flip flopping from step to step. If your group effectively and sequentially worked through the problem-solving steps in the FIDGET/RELAX approach, this map would ideally look like this.

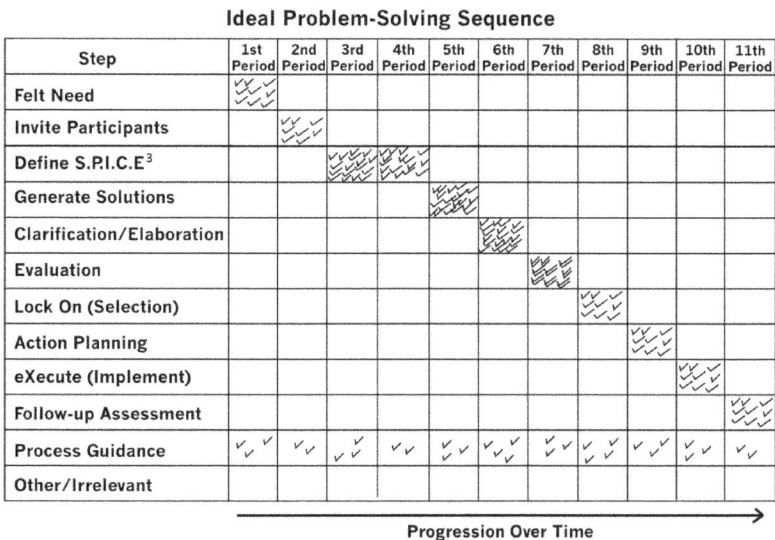

Ideal Problem-Solving Sequence

Step	1st Period	2nd Period	3rd Period	4th Period	5th Period	6th Period	7th Period	8th Period	9th Period	10th Period	11th Period
Felt Need	✓✓✓										
Invite Participants		✓✓✓									
Define S.P.I.C.E³			✓✓✓	✓✓✓							
Generate Solutions					✓✓✓						
Clarification/Elaboration						✓✓✓					
Evaluation							✓✓✓				
Lock On (Selection)								✓✓✓			
Action Planning									✓✓✓		
eXecute (Implement)										✓✓✓	
Follow-up Assessment											✓✓✓
Process Guidance	✓✓✓	✓✓	✓✓	✓✓	✓✓	✓✓✓	✓✓✓	✓✓✓	✓✓✓	✓✓	✓✓
Other/Irrelevant											

Progression Over Time →

However, you typically won't see such a clear sequencing of the steps. A map for a normal but untrained problem-solving group would

181

typically show that the group jumped all over, significantly out of sequential order. This shows that the problem-solver was not able to achieve a functional and collaborative environment within the group.

All Too Typical Problem-Solving Sequence

Step	1st Period	2nd Period	3rd Period	4th Period	5th Period	6th Period	7th Period	8th Period	9th Period	10th Period	11th Period
Felt Need	✓✓	✓		✓		✓✓		✓			✓
Invite Participants		✓			✓		✓		✓✓		
Define S.P.I.C.E³	✓✓✓	✓✓✓	✓	✓	✓✓	✓✓✓	✓✓	✓	✓		
Generate Solutions	✓✓✓	✓		✓✓✓	✓			✓	✓	✓✓	
Clarification/Elaboration		✓	✓			✓✓			✓✓		✓✓
Evaluation	✓✓✓✓	✓✓✓	✓✓✓	✓✓✓	✓✓✓✓	✓	✓✓	✓	✓✓✓	✓✓	
Lock On (Selection)	✓✓✓	✓✓	✓		✓	✓✓✓	✓✓✓	✓✓			
Action Planning	✓	✓	✓	✓✓		✓✓	✓	✓✓	✓		✓✓
eXecute (Implement)		✓✓				✓		✓✓	✓✓	✓✓✓✓	
Follow-up Assessment			✓✓						✓✓✓✓	✓✓✓✓	
Process Guidance											
Other/Irrelevant	✓✓✓			✓✓		✓✓	✓✓	✓✓✓		✓✓	✓✓

Progression Over Time →

By doing such mapping over different problem-solving experiences, the group can learn to organize itself to work through the sequence effectively, build its expertise as a problem-solver, and enhance its enjoyment of the problem-solving process. However, it takes a serious commitment to do such a thorough follow-up assessment, so all team members should be in agreement before starting the problem-solving process that this assessment approach will be used.

HINDSIGHT PROBLEM-SOLVING

Norman Maier, in his analysis of group problem-solving, discovered that performance improved significantly if a group worked on the same problem twice. This comparative approach can be useful as a follow-up assessment device. This second problem-solving effort can occur after implementation using all of the information that hindsight offers. The post implementation problem-solving results can be compared with the original for evaluation purposes and can be used as problem-solving practice to improve process performance for future situations.

CONTROLLED ASSESSMENT

Effective follow-up assessment of the results of your problem-solving efforts requires a careful monitoring of measurable indicators of change. This observable evidence of change should most appropriately be determined by the goal (E^3 desired outcomes) and indicate whether the end goal has been achieved. In other words, the assessment should be directed at monitoring what can be seen, heard, or felt to indicate accomplishment of the desired outcomes. In this regard, follow-up assessment is made considerably easier if clear measurable E^3 outcomes have been defined during the problem definition step.

Controlled assessment of results involves some check to determine that your problem-solving efforts and the solutions applied, are in fact the influential factor in making change occur. Without a controlled assessment, you can't be entirely sure that you didn't achieve your desired outcome because of some extraneous happenstance, normal growth and development, or merely because you desired the change.

In some cases, problems are resolved simply because time passes, people grow older and experience different needs. It's erroneous to presume that you are a good problem-solver if change occurs because of some other variable.

Interestingly, many problems suddenly shift and change once you merely stop and pay attention to them. In research circles, this has been described as the Hawthorne Effect. If you assume that changes occurred because you implemented a complex solution when they actually changed just because you gave your attention to the problem, you will erroneously have learned to waste time searching for complex solutions.

In some cases, luck brings about desired results. It would not be helpful to take credit for the change and feel confident in one's own problem-solving behavior, only to tackle a new problem and fail because lady luck took a dive. It's best if you can assess your results by setting up a controlled situation before you implement your solution.

There are several ways to conduct a controlled assessment of results:

a) Controlled Comparisons

In some situations, it's possible to apply the solution in one situation but not in an identical or highly similar situation. If the situation in which you applied your solution changes in the way you intended, while the other situation where you did not apply your solution does not change, you can conclude that your problem-solving behavior was likely responsible for the change. If the only thing that is different between the two situations is your application of a solution in one and not the other, then you can take credit for the desired changes when they only occur in the situation that you attempted to change.

b) "New Way>Old Way>New Way" Sequence

When you do not have a similar situation to compare with, you could choose to use a comparison sequence in which you alternate trying out and not trying out your solution. If the situations in which you apply your solution achieve the desired results while the others do not, you can also safely assume your solution efforts are making a difference.

The degree of confidence you have in this assumption would have to be less than the confidence you could have in a fully controlled comparison. You're not able to tell whether or not there was something extraneous to your solution occurring at the same time that actually made the difference. You get around this degree of uncertainty by repeating and randomly altering your attempt. With more repetitions of this comparison, your confidence level will increase.

In order to carry out a controlled assessment, you have to have clearly measured indicators of your pre-solution situation, your desired E^3 outcomes, and what you actually achieve. Controlled assessment of your results is a science with extensive procedures for valid comparisons and evaluation. If you are dealing with problems with high cost or high payoff potentials, then I recommend that you consult more extensive sources on research methodology. However, if you are looking at controlled assessment of everyday problem situations, you will be able to arrive at useful conclusions using controlled comparison and the "new way>old way>new way" sequence.

DIAGNOSTIC QUESTIONS

Following any problem-solving effort, you may simply wish to assess your efforts by asking yourself a set of diagnostic questions:

- Did I solve this problem and implement the solution in time?

- Did I deal with this problem at the crisis stage or the growth oriented stage?

- Did I achieve the desired E^3 outcomes? - (the minimal expectations, the exciting results and benefits I wanted to achieve, and within the time period I was eager to accomplish the change)

- Did I arrive at a creative solution – one that is obviously the best, but one that I hadn't considered before problem-solving?

- Did I utilize all available information and resources?

- Did I feel a high degree of confidence in my decision before the actual implementation of the solution?

- Did I enjoy the process of problem-solving?

- Did I learn anything as I problem-solved – did I achieve any new insights about my problem, myself, the skills and process of problem-solving, about possible achievements, about thinking creatively, about bringing about significant change?

Through your answers to these questions, you will know whether or not you have an example of problem-solving excellence. Any "no" answers to the above questions should pique your curiosity and establish a felt need to improve your Insight Solutions approach.

When You Have Finished Problem-Solving

You will know that you've completed your insight-oriented problem-solving process when you have:

- solved the problem by achieving your desired E^3 outcomes

- measured and examined the quality of the results achieved,

- assessed the quality of your process,
- identified any existing weaknesses,
- taken credit for what you've done, and
- enjoyed yourself.

If you've ended with anything less, then you have a definite learning opportunity. If you've achieved all that could have been achieved, then you can confidently enter into your next problem-solving efforts with confidence that you know what you are doing as a creative, insight-oriented problem-solver.

Overall Summary

Problem-solving effectiveness increases when you follow an organized sequence and use specific techniques to successfully complete each step in the sequence. It's your choice – use these skills to increase your success level, or continue to do what you've done in the past. Having seriously looked at how you currently solve your problems and then exposed yourself to new ideas about finding Insight Solutions, you have an opportunity to increase your personal effectiveness, thereby making you more valuable to yourself and others. You also have the potential to be a problem-solving expert.

Insight Potential When Using The Insight Solutions Approach – You may just discover that problem-solving is fun and very rewarding. This might lead you to look for new opportunities to apply your new skills. You may find others regarding you as more effective in life and seeing you as an inspiration. You may achieve results in life that are incrementally better than what you have been used to.

Proficiency in life requires that we successfully solve problems and effectively negotiate change. If the results we get are not as grand as we would like, then it's helpful to take a look at how we solve the problems and opportunities that life places in our path.

However, most of us never really think about problem-solving and don't particularly believe that we could do better than we do. People seldom wonder what could be achieved if we did improve our problem-solving behavior. We get too busy just dealing with problems. There is a belief that we do not have the time, or the need, to consider the weaknesses in how we solve problems, so we fail to develop new skills, techniques and processes to get better.

By reading this book, you have significantly differentiated yourself from others. You have the opportunity to discipline yourself. You now have the ability to work through the effective problem-solving steps to improve your overall results. You can seek out problems, approach them in an organized sequence, think creatively, and identify optimum solutions that deliver results you might not have even thought were possible.

There is logic to these steps – a logic based on how our mind works. This approach includes both creative thinking processes and the critical thinking associated with structure and organization. This problem-solving process takes you from the little itches that you feel in life where your subconscious is trying to induce you to move from the status quo to a better and more satisfying state, through the fidgety creative process where you randomly generate information and ideas to define your problem and find solution possibilities. Then you make a mental shift and switch to critical, judgmental, evaluative, and selective thinking to decide which solution(s) will work best. From there, you can relax, as you identify an optimum solution and develop an action plan for solving your problem.

This insight-oriented problem-solving process can be completed quite quickly when working on relatively simple and readily solvable problems. You might think it is too complex and not worth the effort on such issues, but you can surprise yourself by the solutions that emerge and the results you realize even on smaller problems. In turn, this process works exceptionally well on complex and highly significant problems. You can use this insight approach to achieve synergy – a result that is significantly better than you might have believed possible before tackling the problem.

THE FIRST HALF – CREATIVE THINKING (FIDGET)

F	Feel The Need	Pay attention to any itch that suggests the current status quo is not fulfilling your needs and recognize any such deficit as a reason to engage in problem-solving.
I	Identify And Include Relevant Participants	Determine who is involved in the problem situation and invite them to engage in the problem-solving process with you.
D	Define The Problem	Sort through the S.P.I.C.E[3] of the problem-solver's situation, fully defining the Reality Trough, desired goals and intended deadline.
G	Generate Solution Possibilities	Suspend all judgement, evaluation and criticism and produce as many solution possibilities as you can in a set time frame, reaching for fantastic and innovative ideas.
E	Elaborate	Elaborate on each idea so that the idea is completely envisioned as a possible solution. While continuing to suspend judgement, evaluation and criticism, clarify each idea and make sure that it is fully expressed.
T	Take A Break	Stop your conscious efforts to solve the problem and create a window for your subconscious to force new ideas and relevant but unconsidered information to the surface of your awareness. Engage in activity that distracts you from the problem. More complex and difficult problems will require longer breaks, preferably where you sleep, dream and fantasize.

The Second Half – Critical Thinking (RELAX)

R	Review	Study all of the information and ideas that you generated in the first half plus clarify, elaborate and record any new ideas that emerged during the break. Begin the shift to structured, evaluative and decisive thinking.
E	Evaluate	Critically assess the actual benefits, viability, costs, strengths and weaknesses of each solution possibility.
L	Lock Onto The Optimum Solution(s)	Make a decision as to which solution possibility is the optimum solution for the problem, or in some cases, select a set of optimum solutions.
A	Action Plan For Implementation	Determine who is going to do what, where, when, how, with what resources, and why, so that the selected solution is fully implemented.
X	eXecute	Follow the plan and implement the selected solution, doing so in a manner that reduces the chances and costs of failure.

The Finish - Assess

A	Assess Both Your Results And Your Process	Determine if the desired results have been achieved, and assess how effectively you engaged in the problem-solving process during this instance. Learn from this experience.

Discipline yourself to work through this sequence on a regular, everyday basis and you will get substantially faster at working this way. Your ability to think creatively will be liberated and you will generate new solution options that few others have even considered. Your quality of results will rise and your success will be noticeable.

In addition, this skill set will move from conscious competence, where you have to deliberately think about what you are doing, to unconscious competence, where it just happens subconsciously. When you repeatedly follow this approach, it slowly becomes something you hardly have to think about. More optimum solutions will just emerge from your subconscious when you feel a need.

When you have to problem-solve with others, invite them to discuss how each person approaches problem-solving and find out the similarities and differences amongst the group. As the more knowledgeable problem-solver, you may have to share with the group your perception of the basic steps that have to be completed to achieve insight solutions.

You may become the group's teacher, or at least be able to facilitate the group to arrive at an organized sequence of their own – one they are willing to follow as they solve group problems. Work with them to keep them on track with this process. This will produce higher results.

Then make sure the group completes a follow-up assessment of their effectiveness in terms of both quality of results achieved and quality of their problem-solving process. Help the group to learn from their experience so the group realizes the opportunity for greater success. Help others around you to achieve more success in life and you will achieve greater success yourself.

Successful problem-solving leads to a successful life!

Appendices

The following appendices provide templates, tools and verbal examples to build your problem-solving skills.

Appendix 1: Insight Problem-Solving Sequence

Appendix 2: Active Listening Skills

Appendix 3: The S.P.I.C.E^3 Sheet

Appendix 4: Problem-Solving Process Map

Appendix 5: Examples of Problem-Solving Statements

Appendix 6: A List Of Techniques For Each Step

Appendix 1: Insight Problem-Solving Sequence

THE FIRST HALF – CREATIVE THINKING (FIDGET)

F	Feel The Need
I	Identify And Include Relevant Participants
D	Define The Problem
G	Generate Solution Possibilities
E	Elaborate
T	Take A Break

THE SECOND HALF – CRITICAL THINKING (RELAX)

R	Review
E	Evaluate
L	Lock Onto The Optimum Solution(s)
A	Action Plan For Implementation
X	eXecute

THE FINISH - ASSESS

A	Assess Results and Your Process

Appendix 2: Active Listening Skills

When engaged in problem-solving with others, either as a consultant or as a participant in the problem, it's important that you understand each other. You have a significant contribution to make to this understanding by listening to others effectively. The goal when listening is to achieve full understanding.

There are three elements of full understanding, and you must achieve them all.

1. You understand the other person.

2. The other person knows you understand because you demonstrate that you do.

3. The other person understands him or herself more completely because your behavior helps the other person to see/hear/feel themselves more clearly.

An effective listener reaches for full understanding to make sure that both parties comprehend the other person's reality, thoughts, needs, and feelings.

There are particular active listening skills you can use to draw out the other person and to achieve full understanding.

INVITATIONS

An invitation is a specific request for the other person to tell you something about him or herself. Your goal is to keep the other person sharing information so you learn about his or her needs. As examples of Invitations, you could say,

"Gosh that sounds interesting. Please tell me more about that?"

or

"That's Interesting, I sure would like to know more."

or

"Please explain what you mean when you say (*and then quote using the same words the other person used*).

or

"Please tell me more about _____ ."

EXPLAINED INVITATIONS

Alternatively, you could use the more elaborate skill of Explained Invitations. In some cases, people might ignore your invitation if they don't understand why they should tell you more. The other person might not yet appreciate your interest in helping him or her to better understand the full set of needs. Give the other person a reason.

Explained Invitations

A statement of the importance of the information you need in order to better understand.

$+$

An invitation to tell you more and give you more information

First you explain why you want to know more, and then invite the other person to tell you. For this to work, you need to be aware of why you want to know more about what you are inviting the other person to tell you, and the other person must see your reason as reasonable. Be curious about his or her story and explain your curiosity. Get the other person talking and telling you what he or she thinks is relevant.

For example,

"That sounds important and might influence which solution is the right one for our needs. Could you please tell me more about that?"

or

"It's critical that I understand the real problem we're trying to solve. You've said we have a problem with our XXXXXX. Please tell me more about how you experience this issue?"

Your explained invitation makes it easier for the other person to understand your need and to give you more information.

PARAPHRASING

Paraphrasing is the act of rephrasing what you think the other person means and then asking if you have understood correctly. Give the other person a chance to correct you so he or she can expand on what is being said.

Paraphrasing

A statement that shows what you think the other person meant by what he or she said (your interpretation of the meaning of the other person's words).

+

A check-out question to determine if you have understood correctly.

Paraphrasing is an active listening skill. You don't just listen passively to the other person's words. Also, you don't just repeat back what the other person said. Repeating is being like a parrot. Parroting is annoying. Think of how annoying the kids' game is when a child keeps repeating back exactly what has just been said. Instead, you share your interpretation and ask if you have interpreted accurately.

You interpret the meaning first and then you reflect back your interpretation and ask if it is correct.

For example,

    "I think you're saying that....   Am I understanding you?"

or

    "It seems like you mean....   Am I right?"

or

    "From what you've said,
    I'm guessing you mean....   Correct?"

or

    "Sounds like you want...   Is this correct?"

Paraphrasing is reflecting back the full interpretation of what you get so the other person can correct you if you don't understand properly.

Typically, we interpret what a person is saying based on how he or she says it, what we already know about him or her, our own history, and the context in which the other person says what he or she says. We have personal filters that adjust the message as we take it in. Our values, attitudes, prior experience, perception of the situation, needs, assumptions, mood and emotions all affect our ability to understand what is being said to us.

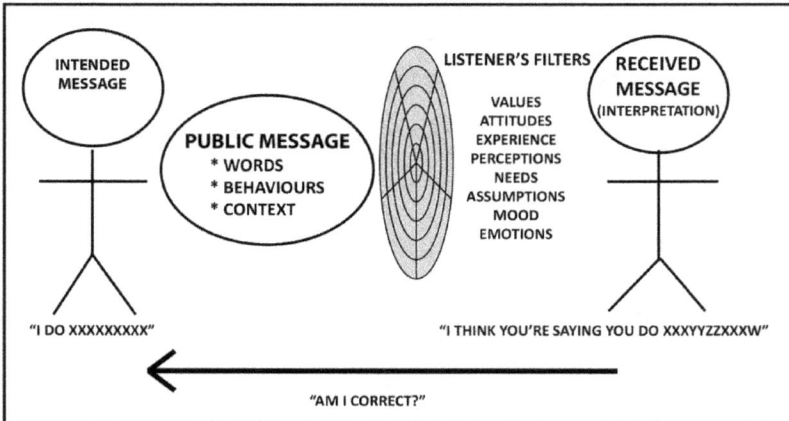

Our interpretation is usually much larger than the words the other person uses. As a result, our interpretation could match what the other person intended to convey in the way of meaning, be close but not quite what the other person meant, be completely inaccurate, or be more than the other person intended but still accurate.

There is almost always a gap between what the other person says and what we think he or she means. So we have to check to see if we have interpreted correctly. The other person can then do one of four things:

Acknowledge the accuracy of your understanding	"Yes, that's what I mean."
Correct the inaccuracy of your understanding	"No, what I meant is ..."
Expand on the accuracy of your understanding	"Yes I meant that and also ..."
Acknowledge your accuracy and expand on his or her own thinking	"Yes and that reminds me, I..."

Any of these responses lead you to full understanding because the information is clarified and expanded for both of you.

INFERENCE CHECKING

To check your inferences, tell the other person what you infer or guess about him or her then check to determine if your inferences are correct. You disclose the guesses you make in order to check if your guesses are accurate, to keep yourself on track, and to learn more about the other person. If you didn't check, you could be forming the wrong impressions, thereby leading you to work from a misunderstanding of the problem.

Inference checking is a skill that uses our natural tendency to form impressions about the other person based on the information he or she gives or shows, from what we know about him or her, or the context and situation we're in. We make guesses, somewhat informed by what the other person tells us, how he or she is dressed, what the other person does, and what he or she doesn't do or say. The skill of Inference Checking allows us to find out if the guesses we make about this other person are accurate. This requires that you pay attention to the inferences and assumptions you make about the other person.

Inference Checking

> **A statement telling the other person what you infer or guess about him or her based on what you have seen or heard from the other person or have heard about him or her, or otherwise know about his or her context.**

$+$

> **A check-out question to determine if your inference or guess is correct.**

For example,

    "I'm guessing you ....   Am I correct?"

or

    "It's my inference that....   Is this right?"

or

    "Perhaps you...   Correct?"

or

    "I'm thinking you want...   Am I right?

Sharing your inferences has the added benefit of allowing the other person to give you more information about him or herself. The other person does this as he or she either confirms the accuracy of your guess, or corrects you. In turn, if you surface something important that expands the other person's understanding of his or her S.P.I.C.E[3], the other person achieves greater self-understanding.

Inference Checking works best when you make positive guesses about the other person, and not judgmental or critical guesses. Use your intuitive ability to form positive assumptions about your other person and then check to see if your assumptions are correct. When Inference Checking, you could say something like:

"My other friends have concerns about maintenance costs. I'm guessing that's important to you as well?

The other person can make any of the same four responses as he or she would in response to a paraphrase – acknowledge that you understand, correct you, acknowledge some understanding and expand, or acknowledge and add the new information triggered by hearing your inference.

FEELINGS CHECKING

Feelings Checking is similar to both paraphrasing and inference checking but is focused on the other person's underlying emotions. You want to focus on those underlying feelings because they are clues to the other person's full set of needs.

Feelings Checking is the act of showing that you have empathy for the other person by noticing how he or she seems to feel.

Feelings Checking

A statement telling the other person what you infer or guess about the other person's feelings based on what you have seen or heard from the other person or know about his or her situation.

+

A check-out question to determine if your inference or guess about the feelings is correct.

You unconsciously make your guesses about the underlying emotions based on observations of the other person's behavior. You constantly attend to voice tone and tempo; watch for facial, body and hand gestures; and notice what is said and not said. Your subconscious mind is always trying to get a sense of how the other person is feeling based on these observations.

Use that natural inclination to add to your understanding of the other person. The Feelings Checking skill is used to determine if you read your other person's feelings accurately. It is also used to help the other person gain a greater awareness of how he or she is actually feeling.

You state your guess as to how the other person is feeling, and ask if you have guessed correctly. For example,

"I'm guessing you feel...   Am I reading you correctly?"

or

"It seems like you feel...   Am I right?"

or

"You're likely feeling...   Is this correct?"

or

"You're feeling ...   about that?"
    (*clearly expressed as a question*)

Your guess is about the other person's emotional state so your guess should be an emotion word – happy, sad, disappointed, frustrated, anxious, hurt, excited, angry, tense, stressed, eager, pleased, etc.

When feelings checking, you could say something like:

"As I listen to you, I sense a confusion about what is to be considered as a symptom of a significant problem and what is just a normal part of your situation, am I right?"

or

"You seem quite frustrated by not being able to meet your deadlines, is this correct?"

or

"You look somewhat shocked by this calculation of your current costs. I'm guessing the size of that cost startles you?"

Once again, the other person can acknowledge that you're accurately reading his or her emotions, correct you, acknowledge some understanding and expand, or acknowledge and add new information stimulated by the other person's expanding awareness of his or her own feelings.

IDENTIFICATION

Identification is also an active listening skill. It is used to show the other person you understand his or her situation because you've been in a similar circumstance yourself, or you can at least imagine what it must feel like to be in the same predicament. Identification shows empathy. This will help the other person open up to you. We have greater trust in people who understand what it means to "walk a mile in our shoes".

Using identification, you remember a time when you were in a similar predicament and think about how you felt in that situation. Alternatively, you can imagine yourself in the other person's situation and then check your own awareness of how you would feel. Imagine you work and live in similar circumstances, you have the same goals, you have the same problems, and you can't solve your difficulties until you get a new solution. Then ask yourself, "How would I feel if this were me?"

Identification

Your description of your own similar experience and the feelings that you had, or your guess about how you would feel if you were in the same situation as the other person is experiencing.

+

A check-out question to determine if the other person feels the same way.

This is a powerful tool you would use no more than once or twice in your conversation to show empathy and caring. For example, you could say something like,

"I remember when I had to deal with a child out of control like you've just described. I felt totally powerless, helpless, frightened, unable to act in anyway that changed the situation. I guess you feel the same way right now. Correct?"

or

"If I imagine myself in your situation, having just realized how much I'm currently paying for less than satisfactory results, I'd feel disappointed about not having had this fixed earlier. Are you feeling that way?"

The other person will appreciate your effort to put yourself in his or her shoes and feel what he or she feels. If you guess correctly, you expand the trust and rapport within your relationship. If you guess incorrectly, the other person will still appreciate your effort to understand what he or she is experiencing and will correct your misunderstanding. As the other person corrects you, he or she expands his or her awareness of real feelings, and this increases his or her motivation to do something about these feelings.

EFFECTIVE QUESTIONING

Be skilled at asking different types of questions. The types of questions you ask have an impact on the quality of answers you get. Open questions solicit larger answers. Closed questions get single word answers. Ask more open questions than closed.

A Closed Question such as "Do you do it the same way each time?" will likely elicit a single word answer of "Yes" or "No". You could easily get that information and much more by asking an Open Question such as, "How do you typically do that?"

There's another way to classify question types – direct versus exploratory. Direct questions seek a specific piece of information. For example, "Do you expect to get resistance from your boss?" This focuses the other person's attention on that specific thought and a specific answer is being invited.

On the other hand, exploratory questions seek elaboration and an expanded story. For example, "How do you think your boss will react to your attempts to bring about a change at work?" This question is more open in nature and invites a sharing of information by the other person that could cover a broader range. This allows the other person to take the story where he or she thinks it should go. The broad answer could include reference to the boss' likely resistance or not, depending on the relevance of that information to the other person's situation.

In general, ask exploratory questions at the beginning, and save your direct questions until you near the end of your discussion. You want an open conversation at the beginning where the other person takes the lead, and a more directed conversation as you near the end. This allows your other person to tell you his or her story without the distraction of your specific questions. It increases the likelihood you will learn all you need to know instead of getting focused on only part of the story.

Questions are necessary but you only want to ask a few. Questions take control of the conversation and can distract the other person from telling you the story in the way he or she wants to tell it. If you ask too many questions, you run the risk that you will not get the whole story. You may get answers to your questions, but if you failed to ask a question about a key aspect of the other person's story, you don't achieve full understanding.

Each type of question can be useful. You just need to pay attention and learn the proper timing for when to ask the different question types. There are several types of exploratory questions, and as they get the other person telling you more about his or her full story, learn to use these different types.

Standard Questions start with who, what, where, when, how, and why. A standard question is an open question seeking an elaborate answer. When you ask, "How do you do this now?", you're asking a standard question.

Status Quo Questions try to get an elaboration of the other person's current situation. For example, you could ask, "How is your day-to-day family dynamic affected by the prolonged absences of your spouse?" This is a good type of question to help you to learn if the other person is not happy with the status quo.

"Best Of All Possible Worlds" Questions ask the other person to imagine the best possibility and describe what that would look like or entail. For example, you could ask, "If a new solution could give you a competitive advantage, what would the advantage be?" This is a good type of question to use to learn about his or her expectations and excitements.

Assumptive Questions start with a positive assumption about the other person then finish with a question that relates to that assumption. This works best when you assume the other person has done what you think should have been done in the situation, and ask the outcome. For example, you could ask, "When you measured the costs of that problem, what did you discover?" or "When you asked your partner to solve that issue, what happened?" or "When you did (*what the other person could have done*), what took place?"

Multiple Choice Questions help your other person to answer a question by giving several answers to choose from. Give the other person several possibilities and then ask which might apply for him or her. When people have choices, they feel more freedom. As an example of a multiple-choice question, you could say,

> "You seem to travel a lot. People travel for different reasons. Some people do it for recreational purposes, while others do it for their work. A few do it for both. Which applies in your case?"

or

> "When buying on-line, some people are more concerned about delivery costs than the time of delivery, the method of delivery, or the tracking of the delivery. Which is most important to you?"

or

> "Some people are more concerned about the reaction of others, some more concerned about how it feels to themselves, and some don't care how it feels as long as the problem gets solved on time and within budget. Do you care either way?

Alternatively, you could help your other person to answer by asking an explained question.

Explained Questions start with a clear declaration of your reason for asking a particular question. This gives the other person a reference point to better understand the reason for giving you the information.

Explained Question

A clear statement of the full reason that you wish to ask a question.

$+$

An open question to draw out all of the other person's thoughts in response to your need to know that information.

To use this skill effectively, you must first understand your real reason for asking a particular question. This requires an expanded awareness of your own motives and your own requirements for certain bits of information. Consequently, you should have a specific purpose behind each question that you ask.

As an example of an **Explained Question**, you could say,

> "In order to understand your goals, I need to know what you hope to gain by working on this problem. What benefits are you looking for?"

or

> "In order to help, I would like to know more about any symptoms or problems you experience right now. Have you noticed any particular difficulties when you are (_doing what the other person does_) ?"

* * *

To build your proficiency at asking questions, know:

1. when to ask a question,

2. what to ask about,

3. how to choose the type of question to ask in order to make answering the question easier for the other person, and

4. when to use the active listening skills instead.

Experiment with different questions and different question types. Notice how the other person reacts. Pay attention to his or her non-verbal responses. If there is any hesitation, or apparent reluctance, there may be a problem with your question. Do you see the other person relax as you ask the question, or get tense? Does the other person move toward you ever so slightly, or move back? Does he or she show excitement about answering the question, or suspicion? Learn to use your questions effectively and you'll be much more helpful.

Appendix 3: The S.P.I.C.E^3 Sheet

SITUATION

_____

_____

_____

_____

PROBLEMS

_____

_____

_____

_____

IMPLICATIONS/COSTS

_____

_____

_____

_____

CONSTRAINTS

_____

_____

_____

_____

EXPECTATIONS, EXCITING BENEFITS, EAGERNESS

_____

_____

_____

_____

Appendix 4: Chart For Mapping Your Problem-Solving Process

Problem-Solving Map

Step	1st Period	2nd Period	3rd Period	4th Period	5th Period	6th Period	7th Period	8th Period	9th Period	10th Period	11th Period
Felt Need											
Invite Participants											
Define S.P.I.C.E^3											
Generate Solutions											
Elaboration/Clarification											
Evaluation											
Lock On (Selection)											
Action Planning											
eXecute (Implement)											
Follow-up Assessment											
Process Guidance											
Other/Irrelevant											

Progression Over Time

INSTRUCTIONS

Tape-record your problem-solving discussion from the Felt Need step through the execution of your solution to the Finish where you assess how you have done. This can be either an audio or video tape. You will be primarily focussed on what people are saying so audio is sufficient.

To complete this map, play back the tape-recording of your problem-solving discussion, listening to sequential segments of your total discussion. Take the total time that you discussed the problem while recording and divide it into equal time periods. Aim for ten to twelve time periods.

The length of a time period will depend on how long the discussion lasted. If you problem-solved for 30 minutes, then the time periods might be only three minutes long. If you problem-solved for four hours, then the periods might be twenty minutes long, and so on depending on how long it took you to work on the problem.

If the implementation period is going to be long, or if the setting for implementation does not allow for recording the implementation period, then the time recorded would likely be the time spent up to implementation and then again after when the group was doing the follow-up assessment.

Everyone should be sure they fully understand what step the different types of comments would fall into before playing back the voice or video recording. The examples in Appendix 5 of problem-solving statements for each step will help you to do that.

Using the map, play each segment from your tape, and categorize what you hear during that segment. For each comment that is made during that segment, place a check mark in the appropriate step and the column for that segment or period. In other words, all of your check marks for the first segment would only be in column one, but could fall into any of the steps, depending on what is said. As you move forward in time, make sure to place your check marks in the column for the segment you are listening to.

If doing this as a group, each person will have their own map and work alone, scoring the statements as well as he or she can. Each person will attempt to do his or her best to determine which step each statement relates to. When you hear a statement or question, decide which step it falls into and put a check mark in that row. Proceed through the recording with each person privately filling out their sheet. Do not discuss each statement.

For the first period, play the first statement and stop the playback. Each person will then determine which step the comment fits within. Put a check mark in the cell for that step in the first column. For the first period, the check marks are to only be placed in the first column for period #1. Continue playing back the recording, one statement at a time.

If a statement is about feeling the need, place a check mark in the "Felt Need" box. If the statement is part of defining the problem, place a check mark in the "Defining The S.P.I.C.E^3" box. If it is a solution idea, place a check mark in the "Generate Solutions" box. Do this for all statements in order as you hear them. Do this until the time period for the first segment has elapsed.

Then move to the second column and play the recording of the second period. To speed the process up, just let the tape run and people will do their best to keep up and score each statement. Place your check marks in the step that each statement falls into within the column for the second period. Do this, moving forward to the next column after you have played back the recording for each period, until you have played back the total recording.

You do not have to agree on how each statement was scored. There will be differences. If the group did not deliberately follow the twelve step sequence, it will likely be harder to tell what some statements were. Without a clear progression, some statements might sound like defining the problem or a solution suggestion or an evaluation.

In addition, some people will string three things together in one statement. "Yeah but that idea won't work because it costs too much. I think we should do.... And Bill, you could be the supervisor while we do it." Some members might rate this as evaluation, others as locking on to a solution, and someone else might see it as action planning. Ideally, this should cause check marks to be placed in three rows in that column – Evaluation, Lock On, and Action Planning.

After you have played back all periods, then compare maps. They do not have to match exactly. Just get a general impression of how organized your group discussion was. Discuss this as a group. Identify strengths and weaknesses. Talk about what kept you organized and what, if anything, might have caused some flip-flopping across the steps.

There is significant learning to be had about the need to improve the clarity of your problem-solving process. The group needs to find ways to keep all members on the same step at the same time. From this discussion, decide what you want to do to improve your problem-solving process when working together on your next problem. Be very specific about the steps that you wish to follow and how you will keep yourselves on track.

> You don't have to use the map provided in this appendix if the group has defined its own preferred process before solving this problem. Make up a map consistent with your defined approach and put the names of your steps in the left most column. You might need to make up examples of the statements appropriate for each step as has been done for the FIDGET/RELAX approach and shown in Appendix 5. Then use your own chart to do this analytic exercise.

Appendix 5: Examples Of Problem-Solving Statements

In order to successfully map your problem-solving behavior, it's necessary to be able to recognize which step a particular statement applies to. Some examples for each step are presented below.

FELT NEED

These statements involve expression or exploration of feelings and the sense that things are not as good as they could be.

"I'm upset about my job."

"Everyone here feels embarrassed about what is going on."

"I'm sort of bored and thinking of developing something new."

"Everything seems so hopeless."

"I think we have some new opportunities available to us."

"It seems that something isn't working the way it should."

"Has anyone noticed that we seem to be making more mistakes?"

INVITE RELEVANT PARTICIPANTS

These statements involve a focus on who else is relevant enough to the problem that they should be included in the problem-solving discussion.

"Who else is a part of this problem?"

"I think Bob should be here. He has the most to gain or lose by what we decide to do."

"Can you think of anyone that might share the concerns that we have?"

"Do you think this is the whole group of people that should be involved in our discussions about this problem?"

"What about Eva? Should we be inviting her to meet with us?"

"I know this will really affect Purchasing and I think we need one of them involved in this."

DEFINE THE PROBLEM

These statements involve defining the problem and specifically address the elements of the problem-solver's S.P.I.C.E[3].

The Situation

"Right now, there are eighteen people working here."

"The typical turnaround time from beginning to completion is currently two months."

"We have a distance of twenty miles to cover in each of our daily hikes."

"There is $3,000 in the budget for this problem."

The Problem

"We've noticed that machinery downtime has escalated since we installed the last software upgrade."

"We won't be able to get back in time for the party if we use Jack's car."

"It seems that absenteeism in Division A went up after Paul was made the supervisor."

"I've applied for employment at six different places and they each expressed concern about my lack of prior work experience."

"When the products are loaded from the shipping dock into the trucks, the packing cartons are being bruised and damaged by the sharp corners of the rear doors."

"You've been late for choir practice four times in the last three months."

"New grants have come available to fund new programs in the delivery of services to the homeless."

"We currently produce 5,000 units per month and headquarters wants us to find ways to produce 7,500."

The Implications

"Sue is falling behind in her school work because she missed school five days this month."

"It currently costs us $1.50 to build each unit because the current materials are harder to get."

"We spent $50,000 last month on equipment servicing because the age of the equipment means more breakdowns."

"I gain an additional $2,200 in debt each month that I'm not able to work."

"Five man-hours are wasted each time we have one of these meetings and fail to arrive at a quality solution."

"It currently costs $100 to process each transaction because it's a manual process."

The Constraints

"We haven't been able to fix this because there is no money in our budget."

"It seems to me that we can't solve this problem because it would be against company policy to do this any other way."

"I think we have to do it this way."

"We can't modify any of these materials."

"We aren't allowed to find a new supplier because our contracts require us to use this company."

"We can't involve others in our problem-solving because we're supposed to keep it a secret."

"Are you sure that's a roadblock? I don't think it is."

"I think you're just imagining that. I don't think it's a real limitation."

The E³ Outcomes (Goals and Deadline)

"We'll aim for an increase of 15% this year."

"I want to be studying in a good Paris art school by the fall."

"Eight out of ten people will elect to participate in our program."

"We need to reduce our error rate to less than 1 in 100,000 by the end of this month to meet the new standards imposed by headquarters."

"I think we could win the regionals this year if we find a way to win the remaining games."

"We need to realize sales of $1,000,000 in the first year after introducing this new product."

"We must have a solution by March."

"The pastor expects our report by Friday."

"We need to be able to build a unit in less than five minutes or the solution is a failure."

SOLUTION GENERATION

These statements all involve making a suggestion as to a possible solution to the problem.

"We could put them together inside a vacuum."

"Have you tried speaking to him about the issues?"

"You might glue the red design on the black."

"We could try pulling the metal sheets through a mangle."

"Involve all three groups in the project."

"Sort the items in order by lot number and then by value so the most visible item is the one that is worth the most."

"Blend the two together to create a new solution."

ELABORATION AND CLARIFICATION

These statements all have the quality of elaborating an idea, either through clarifying it or expanding it.

"We could make this even better by adding an extra bit of length."

"I think you mean that we could switch the two to get better timing of output, is that correct?"

"To me, this idea meant butting the steel segment up to the plastic holder then using epoxy to meld them together."

"This idea could be enhanced by reducing the cycle time by 50% to speed-up the availability of the finished part for the next step."

"Take Bill's idea for processing all pieces after taping, put it together with Fred's idea for using the compressor to spray paint the butt ends first, and we could produce more units in half the time."

"I'm not sure what this idea means. Could the person who brought it up tell me what was intended?"

" I think this idea is a great option that could be made even better by..."

EVALUATION

These statements all express some form of praise or criticism for an idea, or measure an idea against some criteria of evaluation.

"For me, the most important considerations are cost, ease of implementation, and the most likely payoff."

"This one definitely has some monetary advantages."

"This one is four pounds lighter than that one."

"Your idea won't work because...."

"I think this idea is better because it does ..."

"This idea has a major shortcoming because it doesn't...."

"It would take too long to put that into practice."

"Yeah, but it will cost too much to do it that way."

LOCK ON (SELECTION)

These statements indicate preference, make a choice, or imply a decision has been made.

"We should choose this one. It's the least expensive."

"I like the idea about ...."

"We have to pick this one. It's obviously the best."

"These two are pretty much equal so either one will do."

"These two solutions, when working together meet all of the criteria we set out and with the best potential results. I'd go with them."

"It looks like the majority favors doing ..."

"Personally, I prefer this one."

"Okay, according to the majority vote, we've decided to..."

"I think we should..."

ACTION PLANNING

These statements attempt to specify who will do what, when, where, how, with what resources and why.

"Bill you should take the first shift and I'll take the second. That leaves the last shift for you Jill."

"George will phone Frank when the first activity has been completed."

"Sam, why don't you use the spanner and I'll use the bracket wrench when we tighten the ..."

"The signal to start will be the phone call from Jackson."

"Turn the lever quickly as soon as the gauge reaches 100^0."

"I've made a list of who I think could best do each task."

"Jill, call me as soon as you hear from Sue so I can get my part done before you two show up."

EXECUTION (IMPLEMENTATION)

This is the act of actually carrying out the action plan and putting the solution into action. So such statements would be about actually doing something now.

"Okay, go ahead and post the new job descriptions."

"Bill, turn the lever now."

"That's right Jill, it's time to do..."

"George, I'm removing the flange. Slip in the master bolt."

"Okay, hit enter. The update is ready to initiate."

"Add those three ingredients while I stir. Bill, you keep the extinguisher ready in case these ignite."

"I think he's trying to listen effectively so it's time to tell him what you've been thinking about the relationship."

"Sally just completed her report so Jack and I can take it to Bill."

FOLLOW-UP ASSESSMENT

These are statements specifically about assessing the quality of the problem-solving process and the results achieved.

"Oh crap! It didn't work."

"I didn't like all the interrupting we were doing as time started to run out."

"Our error rate has dropped to 1 in a million which is well beyond what was required and even what we expected."

"This looks fantastic. I think it's the best we've ever done."

"How did we do? Does everyone think we got the results we intended?"

"It looks like it worked – the sales are coming in at the rate we wanted, and we have no returns yet. I think we've done it."

"The way we worked together seemed effective to me. We each contributed to the outcome and we processed information well."

"I think we failed to get a satisfactory result because we didn't fully define the problem."

"It seems like we got very playful and brainstormed some pretty creative ideas and that led us to a solution that truly met our goals."

NON-PROBLEM-SOLVING STATEMENTS

You will find that in almost any group session there will be some things said that just don't seem to fit with the problem-solving activity. In most cases, these will be comments that are irrelevant and even distracting to the process.

"That reminds me about a joke."

"Want to go for a drink afterwards?"

"I sure hope we do better at this than the Oilers did last night. Did you see that game?"

"Where are you going on vacation next week?"

"Sally told me that she and her husband were adopting a child from Malawi."

"I'm bored with this and wondering if we could focus on something else for a change."

PROCESS STATEMENTS

In effective group work, it's important that at various points in time, someone says something that keeps or gets the group discussion on the right track. In effective group problem-solving, these are often suggestions about moving to the next step so the group can proceed in sequence, or challenges of another group member for stepping out of sequence and moving prematurely to another step.

"I think we all feel that there is a gap between where we are and where we want to be. If we have the right people involved, it's time to start defining the problem."

"Okay five minutes is up and we've generated twenty (20) ideas. We said we wanted to get thirty (30). Should we continue to brainstorm for five more minutes?"

"It sounds like we've all agreed to use this twelve step problem-solving approach to tackle what concerns Beth. Is that correct?"

"We're bouncing all over the place. Fred just stated an idea and Sue said it wouldn't work. Bill chimed in and said why Bill's idea was a good one, and I don't think I understand what the problem is that we're trying to solve. Could we just back up a minute and make sure we all agree that we have a problem to work on, and then come to an understanding as to an organized sequence we will follow to solve this problem?"

"This is great folks. We're producing lots of ideas and some of them are very creative. Remember to think outside the box and say anything that comes to mind."

Appendix 6: Techniques For Each Step

	STEP	TECHNIQUES
F	Feel The Need (p. 39-44)	• Anticipate Triggers • Schedule Trigger Searches • Obtain Feedback From Others • Assess Your Shared State Of The Union • Ask "What If" • Think About A Perfect World • Pretend You're Someone Else • Imagine Everything Failed – Start Over
I	Include Relevant Participants (p. 49-56)	• Pretend There Is One Other • Present Your Concern(s) • Ask If Others Have Any Concerns • Pick Your Team • Conduct A Survey
D	Define The Problem (Sort Out The S.P.I.C.E^3) (p. 70-74)	• The S.P.I.C.E^3 Interview • Five Lists • Zen Map • 3x5 Cards • Problem Statement • Here Now – Want To Be There
G	Generate Solution Possibilities (p. 79-92)	• Brainstorming • Stimulus Tricks (object associations; change of place; talking to unrelated others; listening to, reading, watching other creative works) • The Nominal Group Technique

		• Get Ideas From Experts • Reverse Thinking
E	Elaborate (p. 96-106)	• Reduce The list If Necessary (Remove Trigger Ideas; Group The Ideas; Reject Previously Tried; Shared Choice of Ten; Pick 10 Practical and 10 Fantastical; Set Number of Rejects with Veto) • Fill Out An Elaboration And Clarification Sheet • Guess At Meaning • Hitchhiking • Visualization • Matchmake Ideas • Take Breaks • Re-Interpretation • Use of Seven Exaggerations
T	Take A Break (p. 112-113)	• Watch Funny Videos • Tell Jokes • Tell Stories • Take A Walk • Meditate • Tackle Your "To Do" list • Spend Time With Family And Friends • Go To A Movie • Read A Book • Engage In Intense Play or Physical Work • Record Problem Related Ideas
R	Review (p. 117-1208)	• Post All Information So That It Is Readily Viewable By The Problems Solver(S) And Add

		Anything New.
E	Evaluation (p. 1264-134)	• The Payoff/Cost Approach • The Advantages/Disadvantages Approach • The Projected Results Approach • "PAN"ning Ideas • Matrix Evaluation

L	"Locking On" (p. 140-149)	• The Solution Package
		• The Implementer's Decision
		• Re-Decide
		• Reverse Persuasion
		• Listen To Your Subconscious
		• Methods To "Decide Between"
		  ○ Let Someone Else Decide
		  ○ Flip A Coin
		  ○ Pick One
		• Prioritize In Group
		• Recycle
		• Examine Your Own Preferences

A	Action Planning (p. 154-163)	• Record The Plan
		• Be Specific
		• Flow Charting
		• Set A Clear Implementation Period
		• Role Assignment Variations
		  ○ Volunteering
		  ○ Training
		  ○ Matching To Expertise
		  ○ Mixed Methods Of Assignment
		• The Big Ten Checklist
		• The 7W Questions
		• Personal Commitment List

X	Execute (p. 165-173)	• Monitor Progress • Implementation By Trial

		<ul><li>○ Pilot</li><li>○ Role Play Rehearsal</li><li>○ Mock-up Simulation</li><li>• Multiple Implementations</li><li>• Refreshments</li><li>• Play-By-Play</li></ul>
A	Assess The Results and The Process (p. 178-185)	<ul><li>• Ongoing Assessment</li><li>○ Ritualistic Checks</li><li>○ Ongoing Satisfaction Index</li><li>○ Temperature Checks</li><li>• Invite Evaluative Feedback</li><li>• Fishbowl Your Problem-Solving Process</li><li>• Behavioral Analysis Via Tape-Recording</li><li>• Hind-Sight Problem-Solving</li><li>• Controlled Assessment</li><li>○ Controlled Comparisons</li><li>○ "New Way>Old Way>New Way" Sequence</li><li>• Diagnostic Questions</li></ul>

ACKNOWLEDGMENTS

My interest in and early understanding of the power of an organized problem-solving sequence originated from early work done on problem-solving and problem definition by Ray Rasmussen, PhD, professor in Organization Behavior at the University of Alberta. My understanding of what Ray had developed was further influenced by my exposure to the concept of SPIN as developed by Neil Rackham, when he identified what particular abilities differentiated high performing salespeople from their more average peers.

Further learning on my part was achieved by working with hundreds of workshop participants in problem-solving courses. Some of these were offered through the University of Alberta, Department of Continuing Education. Other workshops were conducted during the training and consultation services I provided for a great number of health, education, and social service workers under the auspices of the Edmonton Board of Health.

Further progress subsequently emerged during work done by Bernie Spak and myself as we developed the concept of S.P.I.C.E^3 when building the consultative and problem-solving sales model called the SMART selling system. S.P.I.C.E^3 became the acronym and framework for a full and complete problem definition. Putting together all of this work experience and my growing understanding from the observation of others as they engaged in problem-solving, the FIDGET/RELAX model emerged.

Ray Rasmussen also provided guidance on the self publishing process that facilitated getting this document out of my word processor and into printed book format through CreateSpace and the digital format for Kindle. Katherine Caine read a draft of the manuscript and offered her suggestions and edits to make this more readable.

I thank them all for their contributions. However I take full ownership of any errors, omissions, or inadequacies.

ABOUT THE AUTHOR

Gary R. Ford, MBA, PhD

After achieving undergraduate and master's degrees in business administration plus a PhD in Educational Psychology, Gary has had a varied career that led to a better understanding of the problem-solving process. He worked as a lecturer in a business program at the University of Alberta. He worked as a registered psychologist doing counseling with individuals, couples, and families, as well as training and organizational development work with health, social service, legal and educational institutions. Through this work he expanded his understanding of change processes, systems theory and problem-solving behavior.

Seeking practical experience, he then made a radical career choice and operated a retail and corporate sales organization for 20 years. From this work, he entered his first retirement at the age of 55. Unable to sit still for long, he then worked as a Dean of Business with a start-up Canadian university for five years. He left to write and develop training materials on The S.P.I.C.E^3, Insight Sales, Insight Problem-Solving, and Insight Peer Counseling.

Gary is currently spending his time engaged in writing and photography.

INSIGHT
PUBLISHERS

Box 2 Site 3 RR #1 South
Thorsby, Alberta, Canada
T0C 2P0
www.garyrford.ca/insight

Other Insight Books Published By This Author

Insight Sales (Corporate)

Insight Sales (Retail)

Insight Sales (Corporate and Retail)

A Quick Guide To Insight Sales

Other Insight Books Pending By This Author

Insight Peer Counseling

Other Books Published By This Author

intimate moments: A Haibun Collection